A Guy's
Guide to Being a
Man's Man

A Guy's Guide to Being a Man's Man

Frank Vincent

and

Steven Priggé

BERKLEY BOOKS, NEW YORK

THE BERKLEY PUBLISHING GROUP
Published by the Penguin Group
Penguin Group (USA) Inc.
375 Hudson Street, New York, New York 10014, USA
Penguin Group (Canada), 90 Eglinton Avenue East, Suite 700, Toronto, Ontario M4P 2Y3, Canada
(a division of Pearson Penguin Canada Inc.)
Penguin Books Ltd., 80 Strand, London WC2R 0RL, England
Penguin Group Ireland, 25 St. Stephen's Green, Dublin 2, Ireland (a division of Penguin Books Ltd.)
Penguin Group (Australia), 250 Camberwell Road, Camberwell, Victoria 3124, Australia
(a division of Pearson Australia Group Pty. Ltd.)
Penguin Books India Pvt. Ltd., 11 Community Centre, Panchsheel Park, New Delhi—110 017, India
Penguin Group (NZ), Cnr. Airborne and Rosedale Roads, Albany, Auckland 1310, New Zealand
(a division of Pearson New Zealand Ltd.)
Penguin Books (South Africa) (Pty.) Ltd., 24 Sturdee Avenue, Rosebank, Johannesburg 2196,
South Africa

Penguin Books Ltd., Registered Offices: 80 Strand, London WC2R 0RL, England

While the author has made every effort to provide accurate telephone numbers and Internet addresses at the time of publication, neither the publisher nor the author assumes any responsibility for errors, or for changes that occur after publication. The publisher does not have any control over and does not assume any responsibility for author or third-party websites or their content.

The recipes contained in this book are to be followed exactly as written. The publisher is not responsible for your specific health or allergy needs that may require medical supervision. The publisher is not responsible for any adverse reactions to the recipes contained in this book.

A GUY'S GUIDE TO BEING A MAN'S MAN

First Edition: March 2006

ISBN: 0-425-20876-1

This book has been catalogued with the Library of Congress.

PRINTED IN THE UNITED STATES OF AMERICA

10   9   8   7   6   5   4   3   2   1

This book is dedicated to Frank and Mary Gattuso,
who raised me to be a man's man.

"The world makes way for the man who knows where he is going."

—Ralph Waldo Emerson

Contents

Acknowledgments   xi

Foreword by James Gandolfini   xv

Introduction   xvii

Part One: Dating Like a Man's Man   1

Getting the Digits   7

The First Date   13

Tell the Ex to Go Home and Get His Shinebox!   18

Going Steady   21

Part Two: Watching Movies Like a Man's Man   27

Gangster Flicks   31

Western Flicks   38

Sports Flicks   45

War Flicks   52

Chick Flicks   59

Part Three: Smoking Cigars Like a Man's Man   61

What to Smoke   66

Back to Basics   74

* Man's Man Interview
with Vincent "Big Pussy" Pastore   83

Part Four: **Mangia Like a Man's Man**   91
Man's Man Restaurants   96
Your Mother's Always the Best Cook   110
That's Entertaining   117
Salud!   125

Part Five: **Listening to Music Like a Man's Man**   135
Top Man's Man Music Legends   139
Music Picks   148
* Man's Man Interview
with Steven Van Zandt   158

Part Six: **Visiting Vegas Like a Man's Man**   167
A Man's Man Las Vegas History   174
Top Ten Man's Man Hotels   180
* Man's Man Interview
with James Caan   204

Part Seven: **Looking Like a Man's Man**   211
The Looks   216
Getting Past the Doorman   224
Grooming   230
Accessories   237

Epilogue   245
Frank Vincent Filmography   249
Photo Credits   251

Acknowledgments

A special thank-you to Steven Priggé, who through his talent and unstoppable work ethic helped me make a longtime dream come true. I'd like to express my sincere gratitude to James Gandolfini, whose talent as an actor is unequaled, whose friendship is unconditional, and who took the time out of a busy schedule to write a warm and heartfelt foreword. I was very lucky to obtain insightful and informative interviews by three real man's man friends—James Caan, Steven Van Zandt, and Vincent Pastore. I'm very grateful for the support—it means a lot. Thank you, Edie Falco, Ray Liotta, Debi Mazar, Denis Leary, and Rosie Perez for your faith and trust. I'm indebted many times over to Martin Scorsese; without his help I'd still be playing drums in Secaucus.

I want to thank my wife, Katherine, whose vision and patience throughout this project kept me on course; Donato Mennella, for his photography, hard work, and for putting up with Katherine, Steven, and me; Gene Gabelli and Jim Beckner of Gabelli Studios for their time and patience; photographers Brian Hamill, Phil Caruso, Monica Drew, David M Warren, and Adolfo Gallela; Anthony Rose and Rachel Benoit of High Rollers for their hospitality; Jay Tarantino of Flowerama in Belleville, New Jersey, for her floral expertise; John Chibarro for the guidance on the recipes; Lou Silver, my friend and man's man cigar mentor; Michael Herklots and the staff at Davidoff of Geneva, Madison Avenue, thank you for the great cigars and for making us feel right at home.

Thanks to Melissa Prophet for her undying loyalty; Karen Federock Bongiorno for hanging in all these years; Mark Infante, my man's man attorney; and Bill and Edwina Ramal (thanks, Bill, for the start).

My appreciation goes to: Northeast Media Group, Ron Bard and Mitch Ducksworth, for their faith in our vision; the team at Putnam for a great job: David and Elizabeth Shanks; Leslie Gelbman; Marilyn Ducksworth; our editor, Denise Silvestro; Katherine Day; Carolyn Birbiglia; and Paul Dykerhoff.

My love goes to: My daughters, Debra and Maria; my son, Tony; my sons-in-law, Tommy DeFranco and Jimmy Pomponio; and my grandchildren, Tori and TJ DeFranco; love also to Nick and Gayle, Jim and Elaine Gattuso and families; the Gattusos in Florida and Massachusetts; the Riccis from New Jersey; the Garfield Contes, Dr. Dan and Barbara, Dr. Ken, Dr. Dan III and Leslie; Stacy and Carl Susini; Jamie and Carl Kreshpane and family; Goodfellas' head chef, Vincent, and managers Sam and Pam; and Peter Verdicchio of Stretch's restaurant in Livingston, New Jersey.

Most of all, thank you, Nanny, Poppy, Aunt Jean, and Uncle Jimmy for the memories.

—Frank Vincent

I want to start off by thanking the man's man himself, Frank Vincent. It was a pleasure to work with you and to get to know you so well. I always thought you were a great actor, but now I know you're a great person. A special thanks to James Gandolfini, who wrote a wonderful foreword that introduced this book with class. My gratitude also goes to Lina, Katherine, and my sister Dana for all of their creative help when we really needed a woman's point of view; Donato Mennella (www.DonatoMennella.com) for taking such wonderful photographs; King, for revealing his tips on how to get past the velvet rope; and Michael Herklots of Davidoff of Geneva, Madison Avenue, who introduced me to the world of cigars with style.

Many thanks to Ron Bard and Mitch Ducksworth (founders of Northeast Media Group), who made this project a reality; the hardworking team at Putnam, especially David and Elizabeth Shanks; Leslie Gelbman; Marilyn Ducksworth; our editor, Denise Silvestro; Katherine Day; Carolyn Birbiglia; and Paul Dykerhoff.

Appreciation to Alan Priggé; Deanna Priggé; Robert Shoblock; Debi Mazar; Gabriele Corcos; Brian Hamill; Susan Priggé; Daniel Zinn; Lou Massaia; Eppie Ferrante; Keya Morgan; Alex Jimenez; Steve Vasak; Brigitte Starr; John Halko; Angel DeAngelis; D. K. Holmes; Steve Hochmuth; Rebecca H. James; Katie Schorling; Diamantis Nicols; Matthew Paratore; Sal Scognamillo; Bob Eckert at Wine Ventures; the crew at the Tenafly movie theater; Grant and Jill Nieporte; Elio and Jen Lombardi; Mike and Alana DeCosta; Joe and Gina Papeo; Ehren and Lauren Hozumi; Jeremy Wilson; and Nick Jewitt.

Once again, my deepest gratitude to all the above people who helped on this journey called writing a book.

—Steven Priggé

Foreword

The first time I saw Frank Vincent in a film was when Martin Scorsese's *Raging Bull* was released in 1980. He played the part of Salvy, a suave-looking local gangster. In his very first scene where he's walking down the street while talking with Joey La Motta (Joe Pesci), it was so realistic that it was as if Frank wasn't acting. With a musical background of playing in nightclubs and being exposed to real "made men," he was a man who didn't just "know the world," he was "of the world." *Raging Bull* went on to be critically acclaimed as the film of the decade. It was one of the films that inspired me to become an actor.

From *Raging Bull* onward, I became a Frank Vincent admirer. Frank's Billy Batts character in *Goodfellas* is a classic. His performance at the end of *Casino* is guaranteed to give you the chills. Many of Frank's movie performances are what I draw upon to portray Tony Soprano. In fact, I stole from all those guys who acted in those films.

I'll never forget the first time I met Frank. It was in 1996 on the set of Sidney Lumet's *Night Falls on Manhattan*. I wanted to approach

Frank and tell him I admired his work. Before I had the chance, Frank walked up to me, introduced himself, and shook my hand. He said, "One of my favorite movies of all time is *True Romance*. Your performance as Virgil was incredible." When he told me those words, I felt like I had "made it" in some way. That was like Frank Sinatra telling *me* I sang good.

Today, it's come full circle. I now act with Frank on *The Sopranos*. What Frank brings to the part of Phil Leotardo is humor, charm, and smoothness. You know the kinda guy—you're talking to him and the next thing you know there's nothing in your wallet and your keys are gone! Tony Soprano and Phil Leotardo certainly butt heads, but offscreen we're friends. Frank Vincent is nothing like his character. He has honor, loyalty, and respect. In between takes, we break each other's balls. It's always fun and an education.

When we get a moment to sit down and talk, Frank has that rare and special gift of storytelling. His stories are reminiscent of my upbringing. We are both New Jersey–bred. Frank's a family man, very much like my father was—a no-bullshit, to-the-point kinda guy. Their generation went through hard times and it helped them develop character and dignity. They have a no-nonsense work ethic and, most important, family comes first. They even look better in suits and hats than we do. They take the time to dress right. There's an old saying that "clothes make the man." In Frank's case, as with many members of *The Sopranos* cast, it's also what's under the clothes that make the man.

Frank has seen a lot in life. His wisdom can be found in every chapter of this book, designed to be passed on to generations to come. This one-of-a-kind book by this one-of-a-kind "goodfella" is hilarious and heartwarming at the same time. Frank Vincent's a stand-up guy. Now sit down and read!

James Gandolfini

Introduction

What's a man's man? Well, you could be one and not even know it. You could think you are one, and not even be close. Or, maybe you would *like* to be one and have no clue where to start. No worries, fellas. I'm here to show you how to be a real man's man. I'm going to take you step by step so you can act, dress, walk, and talk the part.

Who am I? I'm the guy on the cover. Seriously, though, you might remember me from the roles I have played in hit films like *Raging Bull, Do the Right Thing, Casino,* and *Copland*. Or maybe you've seen the hit HBO TV series *The Sopranos*, where I play New York mob capo Phil Leotardo. However, most people remember when I played the infamous Billy Batts from Martin Scorsese's *Goodfellas*. I tell Joe Pesci's character those famous words: "Go home and get your shinebox!" From those tough guy characters, and from some of the special men I've had the honor of knowing, I've learned how to be a real man's man. And now, fellas, I'm going to teach you.

A man's man has certain traits that separate him from the pack. A man's man is loyal. A man's man has integrity. A man's man projects honor and respect. A man's man is tough. A man's man is loving. A man's man is funny. A man's man is always groomed to perfection. It is also very important that when a man says he's going to do something, he does it. A man's man never breaks his promise. In business, when a man's man shakes another man's hand, it's a deal (but get a signed contract). What is an example of a man's man? A soldier. He has sworn an oath to do what he has to do to serve his country and its people, even if that means putting his life on the line. However, a man's man also has to have the ability to be vulnerable, which by the way, is very appealing to women. A man's man is not just a fighter, he's a lover, too!

As a child, I learned how to be a man's man by example. The man's man in my life was my father. He was strong, worked hard, and acted like a man should. He was very handsome and smooth, and took pride in his appearance. My father dressed beautifully and smelled great—he was always groomed to perfection. As I said, a man's man's appearance is very important to him. Sure, my father had his faults like everyone else, but he was a good person. He worked hard, was a true entrepreneur, and owned many businesses. In fact, as a young boy, I helped him by sweeping the floor of his dress factory. Later, I worked as a mechanic at his gas station before I did a stint in the U.S. Army.

I grew up in a blue-collar neighborhood in Jersey City, New Jersey. Our family was a minority because we were one of the only Italian-American families in a neighborhood of mostly Irish-Americans. I have two brothers, and my father treated all of us kids very well, which is another important quality of being a man's man. I remember one time, I was playing touch football on the street and we were making some noise. A father of one of the kids who was playing came out of his house, got mad, and shoved me. Over dinner that evening I mentioned it to my father. Without hesitation, my father went over to the man's house, pulled him right out into the street and said, "Next time you want to push somebody, try me!" A man's man protects his family. Growing up in the street, you had to be strong and you couldn't take shit from anyone, and my father didn't. That's what impressed me most about him.

Being a man's man has served me well in my own life. For one thing, it has given me the confidence and ability to try many different things professionally. I've always loved music: I started performing in school plays when I was five years old, and at nine, I built a stage in the basement of my mother's house and produced my own children's shows. I studied piano, trumpet, and drums. Soon after, the drums took center stage. I joined a band and later started my own band called Frank Vincent and the Arist-O-Cats. We played to a packed house almost every night at the hottest clubs. During my music career, I was also a studio drummer and played with such prominent people as Don Costa, Paul Anka, Del Shannon, and Trini Lopez. Then, in 1969, I met Joe Pesci and we played music together. Joe and I had a big following and were quite successful. Director Ralph DeVito saw us, and, in 1975, cast Joe and me in his movie *Death Collector*. That was my feature film acting debut and it started a whole new chapter in my life. Martin Scorsese saw me in that movie, liked my work, and cast me in the 1980 Academy Award nominated film *Raging Bull*, and the rest is film history!

When I'm not acting, I am involved in many other things, like screenwriting, producing, and doing charity work. I even owned my own successful cigar line called Public Enemy. You see, a man's man is a jack of all trades, but also a *master of all*. That's what makes the difference.

As you can see, being a man's man has gotten me far in my own life. Do you want a piece of that action? Do you feel you're capable of more in your own life? If you follow my man's man code, your dreams can come true. So, let's get back to basics. To become a real man's man isn't easy. But relax—I've decided to reveal my proven secrets in this guidebook. I am going to teach you how to walk like a man's man, eat like a man's man, cook like a man's man, smoke a cigar like a man's man, gamble like a man's man, even breathe like a man's man! I have strategically broken down the book into pertinent subjects so that you can easily learn all the fundamentals. For example, in the section "Dating Like a Man's Man," you're going to learn how to treat a lady right, from the very first moment you set your eyes on her. Then, in the section "Looking Like a Man's Man," you're going to learn how to dress from head to toe for all the important occasions. Hey, fellas, if you don't look the part, then how you gonna *be* the part? A *guy* just worries about wearing clean boxers, but a man's man worries about every single aspect of his attire, right down to the scent of his cologne, which drives the women nuts. When I'm done, you'll be totally covered.

Now, for a man's man, pleasure is just as important as business, and what's the most desirable man's man location in the world? If you said Disneyland, you should close this book right now. It's *Vegas*, baby, and I'm going to give you a private tour of Sin City. Not sure how to tip? No problem. I'll clue you in on the proper protocol so that when you're just thinking about calling downstairs for fresh towels, there's already a bellhop knocking at your door.

Those are just some of the things you'll learn in this book. There's a man's man inside of you just waiting to be let out of his cage, and I'm gonna help you find him. Trust me.

You bought this book, so you took the first step. Now, take the second step and read it, because then you'll be on your way to becoming a real man's man—Frank Vincent style! Then, if after you're done reading it you *still* don't think I'm a man's man, "You can go home and get your shinebox!"

Dating Like a Man's Man

A man's man has no problem meeting women. In fact, he meets so many that it can become a problem. Hey, not a bad problem to have! But a man's man has a certain viewpoint when it comes to the opposite sex. A man's man is tough yet loving. He treats his lady with respect, but expects the same in return. A man's man is capable of falling in love. Many women today complain that men are afraid to commit. A man's man has no problem with commitment, as long as he's not with a woman who *needs* to be committed. Fellas, it's all a numbers game. The more women you meet, the greater chance you have of finding the right one. And if he does meet the right woman, a man's man will know right away. If he thinks his lady's "the one," he'll tie the knot faster than you can say, "Bada-bing!"

There are certain ways to spot a man's man right off the bat. If you decide to go clubbing on a Friday night and you're home before two A.M., you're not a man's man. If you're home at four A.M., but without a woman, you're *still* not a man's man. If it's Saturday night and you're sitting on your couch watching *Showtime at the Apollo* in your boxers, then you're not a man's man. If it's Saturday night and you're watching *Showtime at the Apollo* while cuddling with a hot girl who's *wearing your boxers*, then you're a man's man.

Also, a man's man is always spontaneous. For instance, if you're driving with your date on a country road and she feels romantic, a man's man pulls over and gets in touch with nature—literally! If your date says she's always wanted to be a member of the mile-high club, a man's man surprises her with a charter flight. If your date wants to have a threesome with you, her, and Rolando, her pilates instructor, you tell her you're not interested. A man's man might be spontaneous, but not *that* spontaneous.

Okay, I'm glad you're beginning to catch my drift on the single man's man lifestyle. Now, for a woman to be turned on by a guy, she has to be kept on her toes, and a man's man continually does that. He does not give away too much too quickly, and he makes sure he leaves some mystery about himself. Trust me, today's women want more mystery than Nancy Drew. Remember, nice guys finish dead last. It's an old cliché, but it's definitely applicable. If you're *too* nice she'll walk all over you like a treadmill. So, it is key for a man's man to have some bad-boy qualities to be successful in pursuing the opposite sex. Women like some bad-boy qualities—bad boys are more exciting, mysterious, and flamboyant. And as I said, a bad boy keeps a lot of himself to himself. Trust me, guys, it can be the difference between just dipping your big toe in the dating pool and doing the backstroke.

I've been a musician and an actor for almost my whole life, and fans approach me all the time, especially women. I was at a mall recently and three beautiful women came up to me and said, "Frank, we love your character Phil Leotardo on *The Sopranos*." I said, "Ladies, you don't think he is too much of a bad guy?" Obviously, they didn't. "No, we love that character. We love bad boys. Your character turns us on," they gushed. They went on to tell me that it had absolutely nothing to do with the fact that Phil Leotardo kills people on the show—it had to do with the fact that he exudes confidence and power. He is a man's man, for sure. For the record, there's a good bit of myself in Phil Leotardo and all of the characters I've played on screen throughout my movie career. That's why I'm writing this book!

Bad boys are not guys who trash hotel rooms. In fact, bad boys are classy, and even refined. For example, even though Donald Trump came from money and a privileged lifestyle, he is a bad boy. Bruce Willis is another one. Bruce and I worked together on a film called *Mortal Thoughts*, and we're friends. I was at the opening of the Borgata Hotel Casino and Spa in Atlantic City where Bruce was appearing with his band. He asked me to sit in on drums, and I had a blast! Bruce is a bad boy and the women just flock to him. Now, it's not just the fact that he's a big movie star—it's more because Bruce is very laid-back and very sure of himself. I've worked on numerous films with Robert De Niro, and women just love him. I got the opportunity to introduce Aerosmith to a packed house at Madison Square Garden, and let me assure you, they are big-time bad boys. Wake up and smell the double espresso: a touch of bad boy is what women like. Here are some of the top bad boys around today:

Vincent's list of infamous bad boys:

- Jack Nicholson
- Donald Trump
- Bruce Willis
- Denis Leary
- Colin Farrell
- Robert De Niro
- Aerosmith (*the whole band*)
- James Gandolfini
- Ray Liotta
- Johnny Depp
- Russell Crowe
- Andy Dick (*just making sure you're awake*)

With all that being said, a man's man may eventually realize he has serious feelings for one of the many lovely ladies he's dating. Hey, some of the biggest bad boys in history have committed to a woman at some point: Robert De Niro and Grace Hightower, Paul Newman and Joanne Woodward, Dave Navarro and Carmen Electra, Brad Pitt and Jennifer Aniston. Hmmm . . . scratch that last one. Anyway, a man's man could eventually be in a serious relationship, but how does he know for sure that she's the right woman to take seriously? Well, there are a few important prerequisites. For example, she's close with her family. She is well traveled and well read. She has a sense of adventure. She loves animals (I have a cat). She takes care of herself. She is a career woman (and I don't mean working the pole at the Bada Bing!). Don't get me wrong, fellas, she doesn't have to embody all of the above qualities. However, she does need to have what you feel are important character traits. Also, her life goals and views should mesh well with yours.

In every relationship, there's going to be some compromise, but remember not to compromise *yourself* in the process of dating. Don't be afraid to make changes in yourself, but do it gradually, one step at a time. However, as you're making those changes, be sure you don't lose your identity! You have to keep you own persona going at all times. You have to remember to show your lady that you have a life of your own. It's confidence and self-assurance women are attracted to, not just some phony schnook!

Men, you've taken your first steps in learning how to date like a man's man. With that in mind, read ahead for advice on how to approach a woman. Good luck, tiger!

Getting the Digits

Let's face it: the Palm Pilot and cell phone have replaced the cocktail napkin and pen. But whatever method you're using, the bottom line is getting the girl's phone number.

There are many places a man's man can meet women and score some digits. However, I've found that meeting women through personal ads is definitely not the ticket. I recently stumbled upon a personal ad in the newspaper, which read as follows:

> SWF (Single White Female) looking for a SWM (Single White Male), between the ages of 30 and 50, who likes bondage and discipline. Must enjoy being tied up, slapped, whipped, spanked and demeaned. Also, must enjoy taking long walks.

Hey, honey, with all that whipping, spanking, and being tied up, how the hell do you expect me to go for a long walk afterward? Makes no sense to me. My point is, some women are totally nuts. Also, a man's man never meets women in chat rooms. It can be a bigger catastrophe than personal ads. Yeah, it's a lot of fun when you're IM'ing with a chick on-line for over a year and she describes herself as a voluptuous version of Sarah Jessica Parker. Then, when you finally meet her in person, she looks more like an obese version of Bernie Mac. That online crap is just that—*crap*!

What are some of the best places for a man's man to meet women? Well, there's a laundry list. In fact, speaking of laundry, the Laundromat is a good place to start. I have to admit that the Laundromat might be considered an oldie, but in a man's man's book it's *still* a goodie. It's usually filled with beautiful young women who are going to be sitting in one place for at least forty-five minutes while their clothes get clean. Also, since men despise doing laundry, there is virtually no competition at a Laundromat.

Now, the next stop is your local supermarket. Have you seen the hit television show *Desperate Housewives*? Well, a supermarket is filled with them. When a woman sees a man's man pushing a shopping cart through a supermarket, it's a big-time turn-on. She automatically knows that he can cook for himself and, most important, can cook for her. Bookstores are always a good place to meet women as well. When you see a woman at your local Barnes & Noble, you know she is intelligent and well read. But, do yourself a favor, stay away from the ones who are in the self-help aisle. Next thing you know, you're acting like Dr. Phil instead of Don Juan De Marco, and that's not what I consider a fun Saturday night. Museums are also good places to meet interesting women, and every major city has at least one. It is a known fact that when beautiful European female tourists visit a city, they always go to a museum. Your local pottery class is a great place to meet women as well. I know what you're saying, "Hey Frank, isn't a pottery class a little suspect?" Go to your local Blockbuster and rent the movie *Ghost* and then come back and talk to me about pottery class. Enough said.

Of course, meeting women and getting digits is also seasonal. In the summertime you can't find a better place to meet women than the beach. A man's man takes care of his body during the off-season so he is definitely prepared to brave the beach and introduce himself to some lovely ladies. What is the best way to get numbers at the beach? Having a catch with a buddy of yours and overthrowing the football—oooops, sorry girls! In the winter, I have to say the ski resort is the best place. In my experience, women who take care of their bodies and are fun to hang out with love to ski. I've got to tell you, there's nothing like cuddling up in front of a nice hot fire, toasting some marshmallows and having a hot toddy with a beautiful woman. Isn't life good? For a man's man it certainly is.

Now I don't really like to do this, but I have to address it because it's become so popular in our modern day culture—*meeting women in a bar or nightclub*. Hey, I know the drinks at a hot club are not cheap, but if you invest wisely, *your* stock will definitely go up! I have to be honest, in the nightclub setting, looks are particularly important. When approaching a woman to get her phone number in a club, first there has to be a level of attraction. If you don't look and smell good, then you've got no shot of even getting to first base (for more on looks, see the section "Looking Like a Man's Man").

There is a great scene in the film *Swingers* that's the perfect example of how a man's man should approach a woman. Trent (played by Vince Vaughn) gives his best friend Mike (played by John Favreau) a "man-to-man" talk before Mike goes up to a hot chick to ask her for her digits. Here's Trent's advice: *"When you go up and talk to her, man, I don't want you to be the guy in the PG-13 movie that everyone is hoping really makes it. I want you to be like the guy in the rated 'R' movie. The one you're not sure whether or not you like yet—not sure where he is coming from."* Mike takes that advice and successfully pulls the digits. I couldn't describe how to act like a man's man better myself. First impressions are everything, and you want the first words that come out of your mouth to be gems. Here are some examples of what a man's man says and would never say:

Man's Man: Hi, I wanted to come over and say hello.
Moron: *Hi, the voices in my head told me to come over and say hello.*

Man's Man: Can I buy you a drink?
Moron: *Can I buy you a drink or do you just want the cash?*

Man's Man: What's your name?
Moron: *Are you Consuela, my Internet connection?*

Man's Man: What's your girlfriend's name?
Moron: *You should probably tell me your girlfriend's name before we have the threesome.*

As you can see, the first few lines should be fairly basic. Don't try something too smart, because it usually comes off stupid. You want to strike up a conversation casually—a man's man doesn't force it. You can talk about whatever seems right, but whatever you do, don't overcompliment her on her personal appearance. Most guys do that, and when they do, women know they've got you right in the palm of their hand. Instead, play it cool. Then, a little while into the friendly conversation, a man's man casually asks, "Can I get your phone number?" Casual is *key*.

I also find that when you least expect it, you can meet a beautiful lady—like when a man's man is going about his daily life. As I mentioned, a man's man often meets women in places like the supermarket, museum, beach, Laundromat, etc. However, a man's man never overlooks the obvious. Fellas, one of the most effective ways to meet a woman is on the street. The first "plus" is that they're usually by themselves. They don't have their friends with them. At a club, women tend to travel in packs, and it's hard to get any one-on-one time. When you meet a woman on the street, there aren't the pressures of a nightclub scene, tons of people and loud music. You're just two people going about your daily business. You're not trying to impress her with your car, or dinner at a fancy restaurant. This is purely one-on-one.

Meeting a woman on the street also has a level of romance to it. A woman may have a day off from work when she's approached by a man's man. Next thing she knows, they're having a great conversation. From there, the next move might be to a café, to have an iced cappuccino, and talk about mutual interests! It's a spontaneous move—but remember, a man's man is always spontaneous, and that's what women like.

Things you want to project to a woman on the street:

- That you're honest
- That you're sincere
- That you aren't desperate
- That you're spontaneous
- That there isn't a warrant out for your arrest

Now, the first step is introducing yourself. One day, I passed by a woman a few times in the street and the vibe was there. So, I decided to approach her. I said, "Excuse me, I passed you three times in the last five minutes and I would really like to introduce myself." If you approach her in a manner that's cool, calm and confident, she will be responsive and not intimidated by you in any way. Now, after you talk with her for a few minutes or so, you ask for her phone number. Sometimes on the street, a woman is more hesitant to give out her number than in a club. I'm not sure why that is, but you can bank on it. If she resists giving you her number, ask her for her email address. If she doesn't want to give her email address, then you get her fax number. Fax her a photo of yourself and ask her out that way! A man's man always leaves with something, because if a woman asks for your number instead, you're dead in the water. Don't bother giving it because nine times out of ten, they never call. Fellas, trust me, they never call you even if they really like you.

Now, when you're approaching a woman, it's important to be persistent, but not overly persistent. Overly persistent equals STALKER! Next thing you know, you're being locked up. There are a lot of pretty girls out there and they actually outnumber us men. So if you aren't successful walk away and go on to the next girl. If she says she's dating someone seriously, you leave it right there. Some guys tell me that they tell the girl, "Oh, give me your number anyway and we can just be friends." A man's man is not going to be *just* friends with a beautiful woman if he's interested in her. Also, if she's really that beautiful, chances are her boyfriend is a fellow man's man—and a man's man doesn't step on the turf of another man's man. There are plenty of other fish in the sea. Just remember, when you're approaching a woman, act calm, honest and, most important, *be yourself*.

Since you now know how to get the digits like a man's man, we can move on. Remember that confidence is the key to success! The next step is using that number to call her for the first of many dates.

The First Date

When you get a woman's number, the first step is to pick up the phone and call her, right? Wrong! You don't call her immediately—after she gives you her number, you wait a few days. In other words, *don't look like you're hungry*. No woman likes a man who's frothing at the mouth.

During your first phone call, you should be very courteous, but also be brief. You're not asking her out on a date, you're just calling to say hello. In other words, apply a little of the bad-boy persona. Now, bad boy doesn't mean phone sex—it means mystery. You have to act like you're *not* that interested. It might sound illogical, but you have to act like you don't like a woman to get her to like you. What are you going to do? That's how the dating game has been played since the invention of the telephone. You just have to go with it.

The second time you call her, you should definitely schedule a date. A single man's man calls Wednesday to set up a dinner date for Saturday night. Plan to bring her to a restaurant where you know the food is good and you feel comfortable. (However, don't get carried away and bring her to Scores just because you feel "comfortable" there.) A man's man always picks up his date. If you both live in a big city, you pick her up in a cab. Hey, you don't want her dressing up real sexy, taking public transportation, and getting hit on by the bus driver on the way to *your* date. So, don't be cheap. A man's man turns on the charm right from the moment he rings the doorbell. He smiles when she answers the door and says that it's really great to see her. He takes her hand and helps her down the stairs (if there are any) and then whisks her to the car. Also, a man's man always opens the door for his lady. Whether you're on a date or with your own mother, you should always open the door for a woman.

Now, I have to refer to the man's man movie *A Bronx Tale*, starring Robert De Niro and Chazz Palminteri. In an important scene, Sonny (Palminteri) tells the young boy who he mentors, Calogero, that the "door test" is the best way to tell if a girl is right for you. Here's Sonny's advice: *"You get out of the car, you walk over to her. You bring her to the car. You take out the key, unlock it, open the door for her. You let her get in. Then you close the door for her. You walk behind the car and look through the rear window. If she doesn't reach over and lift that button for you so you can get in . . . dump her."* What Sonny means is that if she doesn't take the time to reach over and lift up the car button on your side, she's a selfish woman who ain't worth going out with! The door test is definitely a man's man way to see if a new girl respects you. Give it a try. (Just an FYI, if she doesn't unlock your door but locks her own, quickly hot-wires your car and takes off she's not the girl for you either.)

The next step is dinner. When you get to the restaurant, you should have a reservation. However, many popular restaurants like Blue Ribbon in New York City don't take reservations. Now, if the maître d' says there's a thirty-minute wait, a man's man doesn't blurt out, "That's ridiculous, forget it, we're going to Boston Market!" He discreetly tips the maître d' $20 so he gets the proper treatment.

The conversation with your lady at dinner should be of light fare.

Some guys get nervous and start leaking more information than Sammy "The Bull" Gravano. Your best bet is to ask her questions and let her do most of the talking. If she's shy and you have to initiate the bulk of the banter, play it cool. Here are some things a single man's man won't utter on a first date:

- I'm going to ask our waiter if he can make the foam on my cappuccino a little more frothy.

- I've got to be home by midnight or my mother will lock me out.

- Want to see a photo of my kids?

- I'm a responsible guy, so I brought the condoms.

- Are your nipples pierced? Mine are!

When the waiter or waitress comes by to take your orders, a man's man asks his date what she would like and he then orders for the both of them. That goes for drinks, main course, and even the dessert. It is a very classy move that signals you're treating your lady with respect. Another very smart move is to share an appetizer. It's a smooth and personal way to connect right from the beginning. Remember, you want to be laid-back, relaxed, and fun. If you do that, your date will forget to be nervous.

Now, some guys make mistakes on dates without even knowing it. Women are very sensitive human beings, and some guys are just plain clueless! Check out this letter and my response.

Dear Frank,

I was on a first dinner date at an upscale Mexican restaurant and things were going very smoothly. My date and I had just finished our appetizer and were awaiting our respective chicken fajita platters when my cell phone vibrated. I checked the number and saw it was my boss, Lauren. So, I answered. After my three-minute cell phone conversation, I hung up. I tried to spark conversation again with my date, but the mood had gone from Christmas Day to Black Friday. What happened? Why was she now colder than our frozen margaritas? I went from picking her up in my car to her taking a cab home and me driving home alone. Should I have answered the phone? Help me!

Mike

* * *

Dear Schmuck on Wheels,

Ditch the cell, pal. Nothing is more important than the beautiful woman you're with, and you have to make sure she knows that at all times. Also, what's up with Lauren? How does your date know that Lauren is really your boss? Why, because you told her so? Oh yeah, I almost forgot, men never lie. Bottom line, talking on the phone during dinner is disrespectful no matter who you're with. The only person you should want to connect with is the one sitting right across from you.

Frank

After-dinner drinks are a very important part of the first date. Now, if you see your lady yawning at the restaurant after dinner, you immediately order two café lattes to keep the party awake and going. A man's man has got to think on his feet so his date does not pull the famous old line, "I'm sooooo tired." You should already have an after-dinner lounge lined up that has some live music, couches, and a cool vibe. Keep in mind, you want to go to a place where there are a few people waiting outside to get in—or even better, a place where the doorman knows you when he sees you, so he can whisk you right in. You want to bring your date to a place where you're going to look like a man's man.

Now, your after-dinner spot should be busy, but not too busy and so loud that you can't hear each other. You want to find a romantic corner. The conversation was light at the restaurant, but here you want to ask her some more important questions about herself. Women love when you ask about them. You could talk about movies, books, music, traveling, etc. However, stay away from politics, religion, and ex-boyfriends and ex-girlfriends. You also might want to dance a little bit and let your bodies do the talking. You want to feel each other out emotionally and physically to get a better sense of each other. I know what you're thinking—most guys can't dance. A man's man doesn't worry about dancing well—he just moves his body and has fun. Whatever you do, don't get sloppy drunk. You just want to get a little buzz going so you're both feeling loose and comfortable. Remember, a man's man always stays in control of himself.

To kiss or not to kiss, that is the question. When a man's man takes his date home, he walks her to her door like a gentleman. On the way to the door, you tell her that you had a good time. You also hold her hand—it's a classy move. Then, a man's man takes his parting shot. He goes in for a kiss on the lips without a glimpse of hesitation. Not a peck on the cheek! You give her a nice sensual kiss on the lips, nothing more. You do not push to go inside her place. A man's man respects his woman. After the kiss, you tell your date again that you had a nice time, get in your car, and go home. One word, gentlemen: *respect*.

Tell the Ex to Go Home and Get His Shinebox!

I f you are just starting to date a girl, her ex-boyfriend can be like a fly at a picnic. Moping around, still calling her on the phone, ringing her doorbell—basically being a real pain in the ass. Hey, I understand when some guys are still in love they can act real stupid. And if they keep calling and calling and she doesn't return their call, they can get even crazier. If a guy's heart is broken, he's capable of doing almost anything. Believe me, I've been there.

So, how does a man's man tackle this situation? Getting rid of the dreaded ex-boyfriend is not easy, but luckily I've got a few tricks up my sleeve that I'm going to share with you. Say you and your lady are on a date together and you just happen to run into her ex-boyfriend in the street, at a social event, or at a bar. This is as uncomfortable as trying to fit a size-ten foot into a size-eight shoe. It's not enjoyable, but a man's man handles the situation in the most polite and confident way imaginable. Often a *guy* will stand in the background while his girl and the ex-boyfriend speak, but a man's man steps up to the plate and takes control of the situation. He encourages conversation to help clear the uncomfortable air. Trust me, when she sees the confidence oozing out of you, it will turn her on big time! You're showing her that you have no fear about competition from her ex-boyfriend.

What exactly do I mean by "encouraging conversation"? For one thing, a man's man always extends his hand for a handshake before the ex-boyfriend does. This is a very classy thing to do that will most likely catch the ex-boyfriend totally off-guard. The important thing to remember is that you didn't do anything wrong in the situation. You're not taking out his girlfriend behind his back, so, don't act like you are. A man's man is never afraid to be in the presence of his current woman's ex-boyfriend. You're the new sheriff in town, and he better get used to it. Continue by asking him questions like, "How you doin'?" "How have you been?" "What brings you here?" "How's work?" Ask him what kinds of hobbies he has, and then calmly tell him that your hobby is collecting guns. Honestly, pretend like you almost know the guy. Once again, you'll take the ex-boyfriend by surprise and more often than not, he will begin to act nervous.

The most difficult part of running into the ex-boyfriend is when it's time to part ways. A man's man allows the ex three or four minutes of conversation and then he politely steps in, ends the conversation, and whisks his date away. A man's man takes control of the situation from beginning to end. If the ex tells your date that he will give her a call, you interrupt and firmly but politely say, "For health reasons, I wouldn't do that. And I'm referring to *your* health."

If you are just dating, and you go back to her place and she plays her messages and has one from her ex-boyfriend on the answering machine, a man's man doesn't say anything. You've got to control yourself—you're only dating at this point and aren't "boyfriend and girlfriend." However, if you've been dating for a while and this ex-boyfriend is calling her three times a week, you've got to put a stop to it *immediately*. Remember, she's at fault, too, because she's embarrassing you by taking this guy's calls. If she has no interest in being with him anymore, then she shouldn't take his calls. Right? She should tell this guy to take a hike. Many women will say, "Can't I have friends?" Listen up, fellas: Nine out of ten guys never want to be "just friends." (By the way that one guy out of ten is usually gay.) So, let me show you how to handle this situation in a very matter-of-fact kind of way. A man's man is not going to stay in a relationship and suffer. You apply the Sinatra method and do it "My Way." You politely tell her, "You are going to have to stop talking to him because if you don't, you won't be talking to me." Feel free to remind her that she wouldn't want you talking to some ex-girlfriend. It's a man's man's way, or the Long Island Expressway.

Here's a more creative way to get rid of her loser ex-boyfriend. A man's man will send flowers on a Monday. Now, I'm not just talking about a simple bouquet—I'm talking about an impressive bouquet of a dozen long-stemmed roses. A man's man spares no cost. In the card, you write something simple but sweet like:

Dear Kathy,

Just thinking of you.

Frank

Then, on Friday, you send her another bouquet of the cheapest and tackiest flowers you can find. In the card, you write something simple like:

Dear Kathy,

Just watching you through your bedroom window.

Larry

She'll think her ex-boyfriend is a *stalker* and give him a restraining order for Christmas. Problem solved. We're moving on to the next section. Let's go, men!

Going Steady

Here's the scenario: You've been dating a particular girl for quite a while. You find that your feelings are growing stronger and stronger for her as the days and months go by. You've realized that there's something special about her—something that definitely separates her from the pack. The little things she does excite you, like the way she flips her hair when she laughs. You dig the way she smiles in appreciation when you pick her up for a date. You love the way she looks into your eyes when you're in deep conversation. These wonderful things that you're feeling and experiencing all add up to one thing—*a girlfriend*.

Men, don't be afraid of commitment. I know most guys think of commitment as the Grim Reaper. But it doesn't have to be. A man's man does not suffer from "commitment phobia." He strongly feels there's nothing wrong with being with a woman he truly cares about on an exclusive basis. However, if you do choose to go steady with your lovely lady, there are some important rules and guidelines you must never lose sight of. Too many times I've heard stories about couples breaking up because they've gotten bored. A man's man is *never* boring, nor is his woman ever bored. In fact, the butterflies should still be flying around like crazy in their stomachs every time they see each other.

When it comes to being "a boyfriend," there tend to be two types of men:

The Lazy Boy

The boyfriend becomes way too comfortable in the relationship. In fact, he gets so comfortable that the highlight of his day is when he's reclined in his La-Z-Boy chair with a remote in one hand and a Coors Light in the other. Fancy dinner dates have turned into Chinese takeout. Broadway shows have turned into Blockbuster nights. He hasn't been to the gym in months. He's gone from calling three days in advance for a date to just three hours. The fire of their relationship is merely smoldering, and giving off a disgusting odor to boot. This guy *ain't* a man's man.

The Man's Man

This boyfriend knows he has to be spontaneous if he wants the relationship to stay alive. Whether he has been going out with his girlfriend for four months or four years, he remembers to surprise her with flowers, notes, and other tokens of appreciation from time to time. Not simply because he has to—because he genuinely *wants to*. He takes care of himself and works out regularly because he knows his lady loves the results. He also makes sure that he shows her the appropriate amount of affection and attention. The fire of their relationship has been fully lit and glowing since the first day they met. This guy *is* a man's man.

Remember, guys, you have to keep excitement and love in these relationships at all times. Let me put it to you simply: If you never got your oil changed in your car, do you think it would continue to run for a very long time? Of course it wouldn't. It would break down very quickly. If you don't apply the proper maintenance to a relationship, it will definitely stall. *So don't be an idiot.* Show your woman you care for her as much as you can.

Earlier I mentioned sending your woman flowers from time to time. Now, I don't just mean on holidays. That's way too predictable, and a man's man is *never* predictable. You send her some "just because" flowers. Those are flowers you send because you love her; because you were thinking of her; because you had a great date the night before; because you are happy she's in your life, and so on. Women love nothing more than a "just because" bouquet. *What kind of flowers should you buy?* First, try to find out what her favorite color is. If you don't know, here are some roses listed by name/color/meaning. Women know all of this, and it is about time that you do, too. Trust me, she will be very impressed that you're even aware of this type of information and have it at your fingertips.

Name	Color	Meaning
Fire & Ice	Light pink opening to red	Grace or joy
Osiana	Peach	Desire
Konfetti	Yellow with an orange tip	Joy and friendship
Bluebird	Lavender	Enchantment

If you get in an argument with your lady, it's important to apologize with some flowers. Mondays are considered "I'm sorry" days at the florist. But, how sorry are you—one dozen or two dozen? Hey, slipping a diamond necklace in the middle of the bouquet will always help. However, it's not *only* about spending Benjamins on her. You can still show her that you care without going into major credit card debt. Write her a card or a poem. Make her a CD mix of some of the songs you both love (by the way, a man's man doesn't download). Remember, it's about the little things as well as the big things. A man's man should always be aware of that.

With that being said, too much attention and affection can also be a bad thing. I have said it before and I will say it again: You have to give your lady some space. Give her a night to catch up with her girl-friends once in a while. Let's get this straight: I am not saying that she should be out all the time without you. What I am saying is that once in awhile, if her friends want to have a night out with her or want to go shopping, she should go out and have some fun with them. Hey, you could even give her a little extra spending money to be thought-ful (if she needs it). By allowing her some free time, she in turn will give you some free time if the guys want to go to dinner one night. A healthy balance is the key to a happy relationship and life.

Now that you're going steady, you should do the right thing by her when special occasions do arise, like birthdays, anniversaries, Valentine's Day, job promotions—anything you and your lady deem important. A man's man always knows how to put on a top-notch cel-ebration with a creative touch. Remember, a man's man sometimes plans these things as much as a year in advance. For instance, if you really love your girl, you know the anniversary will be coming down the pike. So, what you do is save all the emails you sent each other over the past year, print them up, make a nice cover, get them bound at Kinko's and give it to her on your anniversary. (But don't include stuff like the pissed-off email she sent you for forgetting to put down the toilet seat at her place over and over and over again.) And don't just hand it to her. A *guy* would do something like that. A man's man takes his lovely lady out to her favorite restaurant and sets it up prior with the hostess that when you both get seated, the hostess hands you a menu and your lady the special book you prepared. She'll be *wowed* by this man's man maneuver. The email book is the perfect gift: personal, unique and something you can't buy at any store, anywhere.

A man's man also doesn't mind spending some money on these ultra-special dates, either. Every man knows that women love to visit tropical locations, and her birthday is the perfect occasion to take a nice long weekend with that in mind. The element of surprise is the key—do not share with her that you're booking this weekend of love. Take care of all the details and reservations yourself. Book an oceanfront room and speak with the concierge at the hotel to book some spa treatments for your lady. *Where to go and stay, you ask?* Well, the Bahamas is a top man's man choice, and what better place than the Atlantis on Paradise Island? It's the perfect destination to have some fun in the sun. The Atlantis is a unique and beautiful hotel. It has the largest outdoor aquarium in this hemisphere with very rare sea creatures—women love that sort of thing. Also, there are photographers walking around (not paparazzi) that take couples' pictures at a few key areas around the resort, like by the casino and alongside the fountains. Do not give your woman any grief about posing for this type of photo. It makes a great keepsake, and with the both of you looking tan and relaxed, it will be the ideal photo to put up on the fireplace mantel when you get home.

So now you've learned how a man's man treats the love of his life. It's not too hard to figure out, but let me recap for a moment. Remember, don't ever attach yourself to your girlfriend like Velcro. You need to give her a little space, and she'll do the same for you. One of the biggest aphrodisiacs for a woman is a guy who has a life and career outside of the relationship. That does not mean you neglect her! You must remember to send her "just because" gifts and to go all-out for special occasions. The key is to make your lady feel loved and special while maintaining enough breathing room so that, when you see each other, it is always fresh and exciting.

All right, you're now finally dating like a true man's man. Does it feel good? I bet it does!

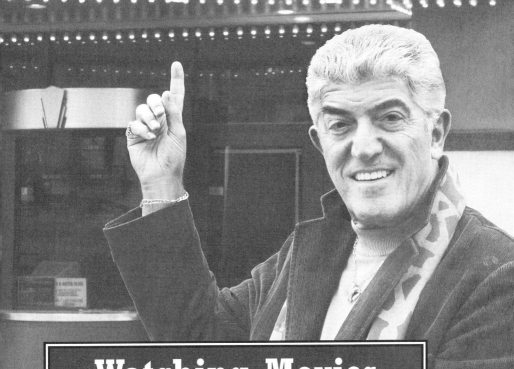

Watching Movies Like a Man's Man

Movies have always been a big influence in my life, and not just because I have had the good fortune of being able to act in them. It's more that, as a young boy growing up in Jersey City, New Jersey, I watched them all the time. It was an era where there was no cable, no video games, no Blockbuster, and only two or three television stations to choose from. Try to imagine ten family members huddled around one small TV eating popcorn while watching channel Thirteen. Today, you'd rather shoot yourself in the head if that was your only option. But that was the way it was back then. Growing up, the only place to watch movies was at the movie theater, and I loved all the man's man Western, gangster, sports, and war movies.

Not so sure what a man's man movie is all about? A man's man movie is packed with action, guns, heists, humor, car chases, and explosions—and a little "T&A" never hurts. A *guy* just channel-surfs and watches whatever the late-night movie is, but a man's man has at his fingertips an arsenal of DVDs fully locked and loaded that would make even Clint Eastwood smile. When a man's man gets together with his pals or even when he's home relaxing, he sits down to a movie that is guaranteed to have more testosterone than a Gold's Gym.

This section is all about the very best man's man movies on the market. We are going to span time—from the classics to the most current hit films. These are movies you should watch over and over again. Movies helmed by such renowned man's man directors as Martin Scorsese, Brian De Palma, John Ford, and Francis Ford Coppola, and starring such well-known man's man actors like Steve McQueen, Paul Newman, Robert De Niro, and Humphrey Bogart. I am going to cover such popular categories as gangster, Western, war, and sports and tell you the top ten films in each. I am also going to tell you the most memorable man's man line in each film. Is "Go home and get your shinebox!" in there? You bet your ass it is . . . and much, much more! Take notes, fellas, because I am pulling no punches.

This chapter is about *Goodfellas* not *Goodbye Girl*, *Bonnie & Clyde* not *Thelma & Louise*, *Pale Rider* not *Whale Rider*, *Rocky* not *Roxanne*, and *Bull Durham* not *Beaches*. Are you starting to catch my DVD drift? Good! Hey, a man's man cannot live on Halle Berry alone! He has a big appetite for film, so here's the winning recipe: You sprinkle a little Clint Eastwood with a splash of Steve McQueen and a dash of Burt Reynolds, and you got yourself a feast of man's man films for the ages. This is a list of man's man movies you can't refuse.

Gangster Flicks

Playing music with my group Frank Vincent and the Arist-O-Cats around the New York–New Jersey area exposed me to many up-and-coming wiseguys as well as "made" men. They drove the nicest cars, had the best-looking women, and wore expensive jewelry (pinky rings, watches, etc.). In warm weather, they wore white short-sleeve shirts with slits in the sleeves and embroidered initials. As a young musician, I didn't have much money and was impressed by the glamorous lifestyle these mob guys lived. Their attitude was another important trait that I closely examined, which has given me the ability to capture their style on film, even to this day.

I guess my reputation precedes me as far as being an authority on gangster flicks. On-screen, I've been put in a trunk, put others in a trunk, been buried, buried other people, shot others, and been shot myself—all that kind of fun stuff. I don't think you'll see me playing opposite the Olsen twins anytime soon! The first gangster movie I ever appeared in was a little independent film called *Death Collector*, in which I played a Jewish businessman who got shot on the toilet. The first movie of note I appeared in was *Raging Bull*, where I played the part of Salvy, a local gangster. I've also had the good fortune of appearing in over forty mob movies, such as *The Pope of Greenwich Village*, *Wise Guys*, *Goodfellas*, *Gotti*, and too many more to mention! My point is, if anybody is qualified to talk about gangster movies, it's yours truly.

Of all the countless roles I've had in film and TV, most fans remember me as the infamous Billy Batts from Martin Scorsese's gangster classic *Goodfellas*. When I first got the script, Scorsese told me to read it and let him know who I would like to play. When I went to see him and his producer Barbara De Fina, I told them that I was interested in playing the part of Paul Cicero (eventually played by Paul Sorvino). Marty said very confidently, "No, who you should play is Billy Batts." I said, "If you think that's what I should do, Marty, I'll do it." Let me teach you the first rule of Film 101: You don't argue with Martin Scorsese! Well, I guess the rest is history. That part in *Goodfellas* is probably the most recognizable three minutes I've ever had on-screen. One of the many amazing talents Scorsese has is an extremely keen eye for casting. Another thing he does is bring "real-life guys" on set as advisors. This is very helpful for actors. For instance, I played the part of Frankie Marino in Scorsese's Las Vegas gangster epic *Casino*. Scorsese had the real-life guy who my character was based on as one of the advisors. This guy allegedly had more notches on his gun than Al Capone. He was in the witness protection program, but eventually left and was now living and breathing on our set! I spent a lot of time with him looking over my shoulder, but he actually helped me in the final creation of the character I was playing. One day, after we wrapped a day's work, he offered me a ride back to my hotel. We walked over to his car and he actually paused to look underneath the hood and the bottom of the car. Then he said, "All right, let's go, Frank." Let's just say I made an excuse and took the bus instead.

Things have come full circle for me in my gangster movie career. When Turner Classic Movies was doing their monthlong retrospective called *Gangsters Inc. Film Festival*, they called upon yours truly to be the host of the series. In different segments, I portrayed a mobster being grilled by two detectives in a precinct. In this creative way, I offered my perspective on the gangster film genre, comparing similarities and differences between the mobsters of the '30s, '40s, and today. I discussed films like *Public Enemy, Little Caesar, Petrified Forest, High Sierra*, and *Asphalt Jungle*, as well as sixty other crime films. The series was a big hit.

Now, I know you want to know what the best man's man gangster movies of all time are. Look no further. My personal favorites:

1. *The Godfather Part II* (1974. Dir. Francis Ford Coppola. Cast: Al Pacino, Robert Duvall, Diane Keaton, Robert De Niro, John Cazale, Talia Shire.) This truly stands as one of the greatest cinematic feats of Americana. I love how this film interweaves two time periods and shows two men's men, Vito (De Niro) and Michael (Pacino). Even though the film lasts over three hours, it's worth every second. Many critics call this film the greatest sequel in film history. I think *The Godfather* is amazing, but I believe *The Godfather Part II* is the best installment of the series.

Most Memorable Man's Man Line: "Keep your friends close, but your enemies closer."—Michael Corleone (Al Pacino)

2. *The Godfather* (1972. Dir. Francis Ford Coppola. Cast: Marlon Brando, Al Pacino, James Caan, Richard S. Castellano, Robert Duvall.) This legendary story of a fictional mafia family in late 1940s New York captured the imaginations of audiences across the globe. I love the way this film mixes mob conflict with Italian-American family rituals and emotions. Aside from Brando's overwhelming presence in the title role as Don Corleone, Pacino's performance as Michael Corleone is first class. An all-star cast of top talents like Diane Keaton, James Caan, Robert Duvall, and Talia Shire makes this a mob movie for the ages. Bottom line, this is a man's man movie you can't refuse!

Most Memorable Man's Man Line: "Do you spend time with your family? Good. Because a man who doesn't spend time with his family can never be a real man."—Don Corleone (Marlon Brando)

3. *Goodfellas* (1990. Dir. Martin Scorsese. Cast: Ray Liotta, Robert De Niro, Joe Pesci, Lorraine Bracco, Paul Sorvino.) Based on the Nicholas Pileggi nonfiction book *Wiseguy*, this film directed by man's man filmmaker Martin Scorsese is a movie you can watch over and over again. From the murders to the hijacks to the extortion to the drug dealing, this film is a true action-packed ride into the world of organized crime. Flawless performances by Liotta (the young hood Henry Hill) and De Niro (the cool killer Jimmy Conway) are pivotal. But who could forget Joe Pesci's unforgettable Oscar-winning role as Tommy De Vito? I know my character Billy Batts will never forget him!

Most Memorable Man's Man Line: "Go home and get your fucking shinebox!"—Billy Batts (yours truly)

4. *On the Waterfront* (1954. Dir. Elia Kazan. Cast: Marlon Brando, Karl Malden, Lee J. Cobb, Rod Steiger.) The realistic atmosphere of the Hoboken, New Jersey, docks in the New York Harbor set the stage for an ex–prize fighter turned longshoreman, Malloy (Brando), who attempts to stand up to his corrupt union bosses. The performances under the direction of Kazan are flawless. Every movie studio passed on this monumental script, but Columbia took a man's man stance and moved ahead to produce it with Sam Spiegel.

Most Memorable Man's Man Line: "I coulda had class, Charlie. I coulda been a contender."—Terry Malloy (Marlon Brando)

5. *Scarface* (1983. Dir. Brian De Palma. Cast: Al Pacino, Michelle Pfeiffer, Steven Bauer, Mary Elizabeth Mastrantonio, Robert Loggia.) Brian De Palma made a classic when he updated the original 1932 gangster film bearing the same name and starring Paul Muni. Pacino brilliantly plays Tony Montana, an overachieving, ultra-aggressive Cuban drug dealer with hopes of ruling the world. But success goes to his head, and so does a mountain of cocaine. His empire crumbles when he gets "high on his own supply." Could you believe that this film was panned by almost every reviewer when it came out in 1983? Today, those same reviewers consider it a benchmark film.

Most Memorable Man's Man Line: "In this country, you gotta make the money first. Then when you get the money, you get the power. Then when you get the power, then you get the women." —Tony Montana (Al Pacino)

6. *White Heat* (1949. Dir. Raoul Walsh. Cast: James Cagney, Virginia Mayo, Edmond O'Brien, Margaret Wycherly.) James Cagney's portrayal of the psychotic killer Cody Jarrett set the pace for a new era of man's man gangster films by emphasizing the psychological aspects of his character. The gangster with a mother fixation breaks out of prison and leads his old gang in a payroll heist, not realizing that his newest henchman is an undercover detective and that another cohort is trying to have him bumped off. Cagney personally devised the scene where he sits on his mother's lap for consultation. Hey, even tough guys have a soft side.

Most Memorable Man's Man Line: "Made it, Ma! Top of the world!"—Cody Jarrett (James Cagney)

7. *The Untouchables* (1987. Dir. Brian De Palma. Cast: Kevin Costner, Robert De Niro, Andy Garcia, Sean Connery.) It was a real challenge to bring the key elements of the hit TV series to the big screen, but director Brian De Palma did it! Of course, he had a little help in telling this 1920s Chicago gangland story from actors Robert De Niro (who won a Best Supporting Oscar for his role as Al Capone), Kevin Costner (as federal agent Eliot Ness) and Sean Connery (as Ness's mentor, Jim Malone). Check out the train station/baby carriage scene—it's the best!

Most Memorable Man's Man Line: "He pulls a knife, you pull a gun. He sends one of yours to the hospital, you send one of his to the

morgue. That's the Chicago way. And that's how you get Capone."
—Jim Malone (Sean Connery)

8. *Key Largo* (1948. Dir. John Huston. Cast: Humphrey Bogart, Edward G. Robinson, Lauren Bacall, Lionel Barrymore.) The teaming of the two most legendary mob movie stars of all time, Humphrey Bogart and Edward G. Robinson, makes for a one-of-a-kind man's man filmgoing experience. Frank McCloud (Bogart), a World War II vet, travels to Key West to visit his dead wartime pal's father (Lionel Barrymore) and widow (Lauren Bacall). McCloud doesn't expect to encounter on-the-lam gangster Johnny Racco (Robinson), his moll (an Oscar-winning portrayal by Claire Trevor), and the rest of his hoods hiding out there. Another Bogart/Huston masterpiece!

Most Memorable Man's Man Line: "When your head says one thing and your whole life says another, your head always loses." —Frank McCloud (Humphrey Bogart)

9. *A Bronx Tale* (1993. Dir. Robert De Niro. Cast: Robert De Niro, Chazz Palminteri, Lillo Brancato, Francis Capra.) This film was based on the one-man show by Chazz Palminteri. The movie illustrates an important man's man principle—never rat. Nine-year-old Italian-American boy Calogero (Francis Capra) witnesses Sonny (Chazz Palminteri) shoot and kill a man, but the young boy does not tell the cops. Sonny befriends him, which eventually causes tension between Calogero (later played by Lillo Brancato) and his father Lorenzo (Robert De Niro). Robert De Niro's directorial debut, Chazz Palminteri's screenwriting debut—enough said!

Most Memorable Man's Man Line: "Now yous can't leave."— Sonny (Chazz Palminteri)

10. *Carlito's Way* (1993. Dir. Brian De Palma. Cast: Al Pacino, Sean Penn, Penelope Ann Miller, John Leguizamo, Viggo Mortensen.) The film starts with reputed Puerto Rican drug dealer and assassin Carlito

Brigante's (Pacino) release from prison with the help of his trusted lawyer David Kleinfeld (Penn). But the New York world Carlito once knew and the friends he thought he had have all changed for the worse. Eventually, his lawyer betrays him, his friend Pachanga (Luis Guzman) betrays him, and the "street" betrays him. This fantastic man's man classic is based on the novels *After Hours* and *Carlito's Way* by Judge Edwin Torres. There's a good lesson to be learned in this film—a man's man should never ignore his instincts.

Most Memorable Man's Man Line: "If I ever, I mean if I ever, see you here again, you die just like that."—Carlito Brigante (Al Pacino)

Western Flicks

A s I mentioned earlier, when I was growing up we didn't have DVDs, TiVo, video games, etc., so, I spent my Saturdays at the movies. I would have to babysit my brothers, so I would take them with me to the theater. I mainly went to the Cameo Theatre on Danforth and Ocean Avenue in Jersey City, New Jersey. If I had some extra bucks, we would go to the bigger theaters like the Loews, the State or the Stanley Theater on Journal Square. They would play cartoons like *Bugs Bunny*, *Heckle & Jeckle* and *Porky Pig*, serials like *Flash Gordon*, newsreels, and two features—one was always a Western. On any given weekend afternoon, the place was packed with kids, some of whom brought their own cap guns and shot them at the screen to help the cowboy heroes win over the bad guys. If you did that today in a movie theater in Jersey City, the other moviegoers would shoot back at you with real guns!

When you were ten years old in those days, you were not looking to emulate gangsters; you were looking to emulate heroes. Cowboys were just like Superman and Batman are today, the only difference being they rode horses. Cowboys, sheriffs, and marshalls are undoubtedly men's men, chasing bad guys and bringing them to justice. I remember the villains always wore black hats and the good guys wore white hats. I'll never forget when one time my father took me to a parade, and who came trotting down the street but Hopalong Cassidy. He was waving to all us kids while sitting on a beautiful white horse with a shiny leather saddle and wearing a white hat. It was a man's man image to behold.

Western movies started to change in the 1950s when directors started presenting a grittier view of the cowboy genre. Great actors like Robert Mitchum, John Wayne, Alan Ladd, and Gary Cooper all delivered a tougher type of western flick that spelled out "man's man." They paved the way for guys like Steve McQueen, Clint Eastwood, and Kevin Costner, among other realistic Western heroes. Pictures like *High Noon* and *Shane* presented a view of the West like no director had ever orchestrated before. Movies broke away from the stereotype of bad guys being Indians and Mexicans, which was typical in films of the earlier period, fights became more realistic and villains started to have more character depth. Jack Palance as the villain in Alan Ladd's *Shane* in the early 1950s set the stage for other Western villains like Sean Penn as the sadistic bad guy in Clint Eastwood's *Pale Rider*, Gene Hackman in Eastwood's Oscar-winning *The Unforgiven*, as well as Robert Duvall's portrayal of Western villains in movies like John Wayne's *True Grit*, his psychotic Jesse James role in *The Great Northfield Minnesota Raid*, and others. The villains actually became cool to watch. As for the women in Westerns, that got better, too! I was never turned on by women in those early cowboy movies because they lived without running water, and I kind of imagined that they all had hygiene problems. Not to mention the fact that they were covered in bonnets and puffy clothing. More modern leading ladies in Westerns like Raquel Welch, everybody's favorite "ten" Bo Derek, and Sharon Stone changed my mind about women in the Wild West!

I have always wanted to play a cowboy in a movie—it's been my dream ever since I can remember. When my idol, Dean Martin, donned some spurs in movies like *Rio Bravo*, it made me yearn to act in a Western flick even more. I'm not alone; man's man actor James Caan feels the same way about Dino (see the "Vegas" section). Unfortunately, I've never acted in a Western film. Hey, with my Italian background, if I acted like a cowboy it would be a *real* "spaghetti Western." The closest I ever came to appearing in a Western was when I did an episode of the hit television show *Walker, Texas Ranger* starring Chuck Norris. I didn't play a cowboy, but a mob guy who goes out West to take care of business. Though I didn't get to ride a horse or wear a cowboy hat, we did film in Dallas–Fort Worth, and some real cowboys worked on the production. Not necessarily my dream come true, but fun nonetheless.

Now I'm going to clue you in to some of my all-time favorite man's man Western flicks. Get a pen and take some notes, fellas!

1. *Shane* (1953. Dir. George Stevens. Cast: Alan Ladd, Jean Arthur, Jack Palance, Van Heflin, Emile Meyer.) A lone gunfighter named Shane (Ladd) drifts into a nineteenth-century Wyoming town and gets a job on the homestead ranch of the Starrett family, Marion (Arthur) and Joe (Heflin). Shane is goaded into defending them and other local farmers from the evil cattle ranch baron Ryker (Meyer) and ominous gunslinger Wilson (Palance). Shane is admired by the family's young boy Joey (Brandon de Wilde), who gets upset when his hero has to leave their Wyoming town at the end of the movie. This ultimate man's man Western classic was nominated for six Academy Awards including Best Picture, Best Director, and Best Screenplay.

Most Memorable Man's Man Line: "A gun is as good or as bad as the man using it. Remember that."—Shane (Alan Ladd)

2. *Unforgiven* (1992. Dir. Clint Eastwood. Cast: Clint Eastwood, Gene Hackman, Morgan Freeman, Richard Harris.) Retired Old West gunslinger William Munny (Eastwood) comes out of retirement as a pig farmer to rid the Old West of sadistic Sheriff Little Bill Daggett (Hackman). With key support from the likes of Morgan Freeman, Richard Harris, and Gene Hackman, the director and star, Clint Eastwood, delivers a one-two punch that makes this man's man Western flick a milestone. The music is also unique and memorable, as Clint followed his instincts and selected jazz great Lennie Niehaus to create the movie's awesome score.

Most Memorable Man's Man Line: "Dyin' ain't much of a livin'."
—William Munny (Clint Eastwood)

3. *The Magnificent Seven* (1960. Dir. John Sturges. Cast: Steve McQueen, Charles Bronson, Yul Brynner, Eli Wallach, Robert Vaughn.) Based on Akira Kurosawa's Japanese classic film *The Seven Samurai*, this movie directed by John Sturges resets the story in Mexico and features a group of then relatively unknown man's man actors. The "Magnificent Seven" set out to seek and destroy a cruel Mexican bandit leader (Wallach) and his nasty outlaw gang. Eli Wallach is at his maniacal acting best and helps to make this film a man's man movie for the ages.

Most Memorable Man's Man Line: "It looks like a few more than we planned on."—Vin (Steve McQueen)

4. *The Good, the Bad and the Ugly* (1966. Dir. Sergio Leone. Cast: Clint Eastwood, Lee Van Cleef, Eli Wallach.) The final installment of director Sergio Leone's *Dollars* trilogy helped cement man's man actor Clint Eastwood as a worldwide superstar. The three western rogues of the title, Eastwood as "the good," Lee Van Cleef as "the bad," and Eli Wallach as "the ugly," perform a three-way duel in a deserted old graveyard. Squinting eyes staring each other down, quick cuts of hands reaching for guns, and Ennio Morricone's amazing score established this as one of the most tense man's man moments in film history.

Most Memorable Man's Man Line: "I like big fat men like you. When they fall they make more noise."—Tuco (Eli Wallach)

5. *High Noon* (1952. Dir. Fred Zinnemann. Cast: Gary Cooper, Thomas Mitchell, Lloyd Bridges, Grace Kelly.) Gary Cooper made the starring role in *High Noon* the ultimate "Cooper Part," reflecting all the "strong, silent type" acting characteristics he became famous for. As retiring Marshal Will Kane, Cooper had to face outlaw Frank Miller (Ian McDonald) and his goons before leaving town with his new bride (Grace Kelly). Cooper acts the part of the ultimate man's man as he is forced to face the outlaws alone after all the locals chicken out of supporting him in the crunch.

Most Memorable Man's Man Line: "Quit pushin' me, Harv. I'm tired of being pushed."—Marshal Will Kane (Gary Cooper)

6. *Pale Rider* (1985. Dir. Clint Eastwood. Cast: Clint Eastwood, Michael Moriarty, Carrie Snodgress, Chris Penn.) With Clint Eastwood starring in the title role as "the preacher," this movie (also directed by Eastwood) has been favorably compared with *Shane*. As a mysterious stranger who rides into a California gold rush town, Eastwood finds himself siding with some hardworking gold prospectors against the brutal head of a mining syndicate. Roughing up the syndicate boss's bully son (Penn) leads to a showdown between the preacher and evil mining boss (John Russell) and his gang of hired guns. Eastwood gets into "man's man mode" as he rids the town of all the bad guys before getting on his horse and moving on.

Most Memorable Man's Man Line: "If you're waiting for a woman to make up her mind, you may have a long wait."—Preacher (Clint Eastwood)

7. *True Grit* (1969. Dir. Henry Hathaway. Cast: John Wayne, Glen Campbell, Kim Darby, Robert Duvall.) When hard-working Marshall "Rooster" Cogburn (an Oscar-winning performance by John Wayne) takes a young girl's (Darby) side against outlaws who killed her father, watch out bad guys! Ned Pepper (Duvall) and his boys all bite the dust in one of the most classic shoot-out scenes of all time, as man's man "Duke" Wayne takes out the opposition.

Most Memorable Man's Man Line: "Fill your hand, you son of bitch!"—Marshall "Rooster" Cogburn (John Wayne)

8. *My Darling Clementine* (1946. Dir. John Ford. Cast: Henry Fonda, Linda Darnell, Victor Mature, Cathy Downs, Walter Brennan.) One of the things that puts this movie a whole notch above the other retellings of the famous gunfight at the O.K. Corral (like John Sturges's 1957 version with Burt Lancaster and Kirk Douglas) is that director John Ford actually knew Wyatt Earp and used his real stories to retell the famous event. Now that's what I call retelling a story like a man's man! Henry Fonda as Earp and Victor Mature as Doc Holliday are great, but the true "scene stealer" is Walter Brennan as Old Man Clanton, who is chilling and evil, not folksy like he first seems. However, he goes down with the rest of the Clantons in the gunfight scene.

Most Memorable Man's Man Line: "What kind of town is this, anyway? Excuse me, ma'am. A man can't get a shave without gettin' his head blown off?"—Wyatt Earp (Henry Fonda)

9. *Young Guns* (1988. Dir. Christopher Cain. Cast: Emilio Estevez, Kiefer Sutherland, Lou Diamond Phillips, Charlie Sheen, Dermot Mulroney, Jack Palance.) This flick features a great cast of then young and up-and-coming man's man actors. A businessman in the Wild West teaches a group of young criminals how to live life on the straight and narrow. However, when their mentor gets killed, they go back to their old ways to seek revenge. Emilio Estevez does an incredible job portraying Billy the Kid.

Most Memorable Man's Man Line: "Alex, if you stay they're gonna kill you. And then I'm gonna have to go around and kill the guys who killed you. That's a lot of killing."—William H. Bonney (Emilio Estevez)

10. *Bandolero!* (1968. Dir. Andrew V. McLaglen. Cast: Dean Martin, James Stewart, Raquel Welch.) "Rat Pack" fans usually associate

Dean Martin with the hip movies he made with fellow man's man Rat Pack leader Frank Sinatra—*Ocean's 11, Some Came Running, Robin and the 7 Hoods*, and many more. But, "Dino" made a group of Western movies without Sinatra that stand on their own. *Bandolero!* brought Dean together with James Stewart as two brothers who Mexican banditos make the mistake of messing with in Texas. Feisty and sexy leading lady Raquel Welch proved to Dino and Jimmy that the Old Wild West could, in fact, be "wild" in many ways!

Most Memorable Man's Man Line: "You just walked into a bank and helped yourself to ten thousand dollars 'cause it seemed like the thing to do?"—Dee Bishop (Dean Martin)

Sports Flicks

I have always been a big sports fan. Whenever my father took me to Yankee Stadium as a young boy, it was always a treat. Seeing man's man ballplayer #7 Mickey Mantle play in person always took my breath away. "The Mick" and Joe DiMaggio were the greatest ballplayers to ever live. My father was also an avid boxing fan and he took me to many fights. I have to say that the day I met Muhammad Ali was one of the greatest days of my life.

As a child, I emulated my sports heroes. The street was our playground, and with a pink high-bouncer ball, we played every kind of ball game imaginable—stick, box, curb, you name it. While I certainly had the coordination to play, I never had professional aspirations. Eventually, my passion for music took over and I focused my sights on a career in the arts. But I've always loved playing sports and often I miss it. I lived, and still live, vicariously through sports movies.

It is my honor to say that I acted in one of the greatest sports movies of all time, *Raging Bull*. As I said before, I had acted in one previous film called *Death Collector*. Martin Scorsese saw my work in that and I got a call from my agent to audition for *Raging Bull*. At the time, I had a full mustache and an Afro haircut (it was stylish back then). I went up to a hotel on Central Park West and was greeted at the door by a production assistant who escorted me into a suite, where I came face to face with Robert De Niro. I said, "Hello Bob, I loved you in *The Deer Hunter*." He said, "I loved you in *Death Collector*." Soon after, Martin Scorsese and Joe Pesci arrived. Joe and I read through the scene where we walk down the street, which was ultimately used in the film. A week later, I got a call to come in and to do a screen test. They asked me to shave off my mustache, which I had had for ten years. They cut my hair at the studio and put me in a 1950s suit and I proceeded to do a screen test for the role of Salvy. Honestly, I was never nervous. A man's man always faces a challenge head-on. The next day, I left for a vacation to California. While traveling through the desert with some friends on the way from San Diego to Las Vegas, I called my agent and he told me I got the job. I was thrilled! We proceeded to Las Vegas and stayed up three days straight, partying like men's men. Being cast in *Raging Bull* started a whole new chapter in my life. The film went on to be nominated for eight Academy Awards and De Niro won the Oscar for Best Actor for the role of boxing legend Jake La Motta. To top it off, *Raging Bull* would eventually be hailed by almost all critics as the film of the decade. Hey, not a bad way to start an acting career!

Okay, so what are some real man's man sports movies? Before I present my top picks, here are the top five sports movies that you would never, I mean *never*, see a man's man watching:

NON–MAN'S MAN SPORTS FLICKS

- *Ice Castles* (1978): Men don't watch women ice skaters, they only date them.

- *A League of Their Own* (1992): Mantle and Ruth are replaced by Geena Davis and Rosie O'Donnell? Enough said.

- *Best in Show* (2000): A guy watching a movie about a dog show? Definitely suspect.

- *The Bad News Bears Go to Japan* (1978): Mu shoo pork and pitching?

- *Air Bud* (1997): A basketball-playing dog? The tagline is: "He sits. He stays. He shoots. He scores." How about he just gives me back the $4.85 I just spent renting this bomb!

Thank goodness that's over. Now we're going to cover films that capture the action of sports and the feeling of winning like no other movies, films that make you want to knock someone out (*Rocky*), win big at pool (*The Hustler*), hit a home run like "The Iron Horse" Lou Gerhig (*The Pride of the Yankees*), and hit a grand slam in the bedroom with a woman as beautiful as Susan Sarandon (*Bull Durham*). *Madone!* There is truly something for everyone on my list of man's man sports flicks.

1. *Raging Bull* (1980. Dir. Martin Scorsese. Cast: Robert De Niro, Joe Pesci, Cathy Moriarty, Frank Vincent—yours truly.) This classic Oscar-nominated film is based on the real-life of Italian bruiser and Bronx native Jake La Motta. The paranoid boxer La Motta is convinced that everyone is screwing his wife—including his own brother, Joey (Pesci). Scorsese masterfully shoots the fight sequences with exploding flashbulbs, flying blood, and explosive punches that suck you in. The blood dripping off the ring rope during the final fight between La Motta and Sugar Ray Robinson is pure poetry. Also, the transformation of Robert De Niro's physical appearance from ripped-lean fighter to bloated, overweight drunk is incredible. *Raging Bull* is the ultimate man's man sports film because it shows not just the triumphs of being a world-champion boxer, but also the tribulations.

Most Memorable Man's Man Line: "You never got me down, Ray! You hear me? You never got me down."—Jake La Motta (Robert De Niro)

2. *Rocky* (1976. Dir. John G. Avildsen. Cast: Sylvester Stallone, Talia Shire, Burt Young, Carl Weathers, Burgess Meredith.) The first of five installments, this is the story about a Philadelphia boxer beyond his prime who gets a shot at the title held by Apollo Creed (Weathers). In moments of self-doubt, Rocky Balboa (Stallone) is pushed by his veteran trainer Mickey (Meredith), who by the end of the movie becomes more like a father. Stallone was also the ultimate man's man behind the scenes, as he rejected countless lucrative offers to sell his self-written script because the then-unkown actor was determined to star in the picture. Stallone was ultimately nominated for an Academy Award for his acting performance!

Most Memorable Man's Man Line: "Yo, Adrian!"—Rocky Balboa (Sylvester Stallone)

3. *The Hustler* (1961. Dir. Robert Rossen. Cast: Paul Newman, Jackie Gleason, Piper Laurie, George C. Scott, Vincent Gardenia.) This is the story of "Fast" Eddie Felson (Newman), a small-time pool hustler who challenges the legendary pool player Minnesota Fats (Gleason) to a high-stakes game. Felson is off to a hot start making amazing shot after amazing shot. However, when the alcohol shows up, the game switches gears in favor of Fats. After a devastating loss, Felson is determined to get back on top. He eventually gets another shot at Fats for one of the most memorable man's man pool games in film history.

Most Memorable Man's Man Line: "I am the best you ever seen, Fats. I'm the best there is. Even if you beat me, I'm still the best." —"Fast" Eddie Felson (Paul Newman)

4. *Hoosiers* (1986. Dir. David Anspaugh. Cast: Gene Hackman, Barbara Hershey, Dennis Hopper, Sheb Wooley, Fern Persons.) This classic man's man movie is all about redemption. Norman Dale (Hackman) is a volatile alcoholic basketball coach who was once the town's star player. Defying all odds, Coach Dale takes his squad, an unlikely candidate, for an Indiana state championship run that will blow you away! The story is inspired by the Milan Indians' victory in the 1954 Indiana State Championship.

Most Memorable Man's Man Line: "If you put your effort and concentration into playing to your potential, to be the best you can be, I don't care what the scoreboard says at the end of the game. In my book, we're gonna be winners."—Coach Norman Dale (Gene Hackman)

5. *Chariots of Fire* (1981. Dir. Hugh Hudson. Cast: Ben Cross, Ian Charleson, Ian Holm, Alice Krige.) The man's man theme music to the film, masterfully done by Vangelis, has become one of the most famous sports songs in film history. The movie revolves around a Jewish sprinter named Harold Abrahams (Ben Cross) and his devout Christian opposition Eric Liddell (Ian Charleson) who compete in the 1924 Olympics in Paris. One is compelled by his love of God and the other by his hatred of anti-semitism. Sports, drama, and great filmmaking make this man's man movie win the race!

Most Memorable Man's Man Line: "If I can't win, I won't race!" —Harold Abrahams (Ben Cross)

6. *The Pride of the Yankees* (1942. Dir. Sam Wood. Cast: Gary Cooper, Teresa Wright, Babe Ruth, Walter Brennan.) Gary Cooper's role as baseball's legendary Lou Gehrig established the actor as a megastar in Hollywood. The scene where Cooper re-creates Gehrig's moving speech in Yankee Stadium as his career was cut short by ALS stands as a high-water mark in sports movie history. Theresa Wright portrays Lou's heroic wife, Eleanor; Walter Brennan, and Babe Ruth as himself contribute to this great American story.

Most Memorable Man's Man Line: "Today, I consider myself the luckiest man on the face of the earth."—Lou Gehrig (Gary Cooper)

7. *Bull Durham* (1988. Dir. Ron Shelton. Cast: Susan Sarandon, Tim Robbins, Kevin Costner, Trey Wilson.) Annie Savoy (Sarandon) is the type of woman whom a man's man does not mind hanging around the locker room. Every season, she picks a lucky player on the Durham Bulls baseball team to share her wisdom, but more important, her bed. This season, she chooses Ebby Calvin "Nuke" LaLoosh (Robbins) whose brain is a few apples short of a bushel. But she realizes that the veteran ball player Crash Davis (Costner) would have been the more stimulating choice in the bed and the brain. All men's men love the steamy sex scenes between Sarandon's and Costner's characters.

Most Memorable Man's Man Line: "Man, that ball got outta here in a hurry. I mean, anything that travels that far oughta have a damn stewardess on it, don't you think?"—Crash Davis (Kevin Costner)

8. *Caddyshack* (1980. Dir. Harold Ramis. Cast: Chevy Chase, Rodney Dangerfield, Ted Knight, Bill Murray.) Not since Dean Martin and Jerry Lewis's *The Caddy* some thirty years earlier has any movie poked so much fun at golf. The setting is the wacky Bushwood Country Club, where an assortment of zany characters sets a frantic pace. There's loud, vulgar, extremely rich member Al Czervik (Dangerfield), gopher-hunting groundskeeper Carl (Murray), obnoxious club president Judge Smaills (Knight), laid-back playboy president Ty Webb (Chase), and other funny golfing types. This is a hilarious must-see man's man golfing flick directed by Harold Ramis (*Ghostbusters* and *Stripes*).

Most Memorable Man's Man Line: "Oh, this your wife, huh? A lovely lady. Hey baby, you must've been something before electricity."—Al Czervik (Rodney Dangerfield)

9. *North Dallas Forty* (1979. Dir. Ted Kotcheff. Cast: Nick Nolte, Mac Davis, Charles Durning, Dayle Haddon.) This man's man pro football flick is strictly from the "no pain, no gain" school of hard knocks football movies. An unusual take on the professional gridiron world, the film focuses on labor abuses in pro football and is ranked by critics and players as one of the best football films ever made. This movie is loosely based on the Dallas Cowboys team of the early 1970s.

Most Memorable Man's Man Line: "This is national TV. So don't pick your noses or scratch your nuts."—Coach Johnson (Charles Durning)

10. *Seabiscuit* (2003. Dir. Gary Ross. Cast: Tobey Maguire, Jeff Bridges, Chris Cooper, William H. Macy.) This Depression-era true story of one of the most famous horses in all of horseracing history is a must-see. An ex–prize fighter Red Pollard (Maguire) and horse trainer Tom Smith (Cooper) team up with self-made millionaire Charles Howard (Bridges) and his undersized horse with an over-sized heart. As a team, they bring the larger-than-life Seabiscuit to incredible heights of success as the nation cheers on this unlikely hero. Also, William H. Macy plays a great sleazy radio announcer.

Most Memorable Man's Man Line: "You know, everybody thinks we found this broken-down horse and fixed him. But we didn't. He fixed us; every one of us. And I guess in a way, we kinda fixed each other, too."—Red Pollard (Tobey Maguire)

War Flicks

There are not a lot of good things you can say about war. However, there are a lot of good films that have been made depicting the wars throughout our modern history. The ones that impressed me the most are the ones that document the events of the last century. A lot of stars made their bones in war movies: people like George C. Scott, Robert De Niro, Steve McQueen, Christopher Walken, and Martin Sheen, just to name a few men's men.

I remember seeing a lot of war movies when I was a kid, among them *Sands of Iwo Jima* (for which John Wayne received his first Academy Award nomination) and *From Here to Eternity* (Frank Sinatra's Academy Award–winning role). We looked at soldiers as heroes when I was growing up, and my pals and I used to "play war" in the streets. We used any situation as a setting for our kids'-style war games. I remember one huge snowstorm from my childhood like it was yesterday. Snow fell in Jersey City for days and days, just like it did in the Battle of the Bulge during World War II. It piled at least three feet high, perfect to build snow forts and create our own battle scenes. We emulated our heroes from the war movies like James Stewart, Richard Widmark, Henry Fonda, and Errol Flynn, as we launched our attack on the kids from the next block. My brother and I would throw snowballs like hand grenades and use our sleds as tanks. There were only two things that would get us to stop playing: my mother's hot chocolate and the O'Neill twin sisters down the block. Talk about snow bunnies!

I did a stint in the army when I got called to active duty during the Berlin Crisis. President John F. Kennedy called up 150,000 troops. At that time, I was in the control group of the United States Army Reserves and my name got picked out of a hat. They sent me a letter to report to Fort Dix in two weeks. I was married, had a daughter, and was playing music in clubs, but hey, when Uncle Sam rang, you answered. I learned a lot from my time in the service. I learned about patriotism and respect for my country. There was a lot of camaraderie between soldiers and to overcome the tension of possibly being sent overseas there were a lot of jokers in the unit. I'll never forget the time a few guys in the next barracks nailed some smart-ass sergeant's combat boots to the floor for giving them a hard time. Did you ever try to put boots on in a hurry, only to find that they are nailed to the floor? Those are the things you don't usually see on the screen, unless you happen to be watching *M*A*S*H*.

Let's face it, war movies made right after serious conflicts like Vietnam, Korea, World War II, etc., didn't reflect much humor. What they did reflect was inspiration and a better grasp of what it was like for our troops to fight for *our* freedom. In my list below you will see some of the most influential and well-made war movies of all time. Movies that epitomize what a man's man is all about. Why do we want to be like the soldiers we see on film? Soldiers are strong, daring, patriotic and, most important . . . women love men in uniform!

1. *Patton* (1970. Dir. Franklin J. Schaffner. Cast: George C. Scott, Karl Malden, Stephen Young, Michael Strong, Carey Loftin.) Nicknamed "Old Blood and Guts," General George Patton came alive on the movie screen in the form of George C. Scott's memorable man's man Academy Award–winning performance as the legendary World War II leader. A fascinating personality, Patton believed he was an eighteenth-century general living in the modern era, and Scott developed all the nuances of this complex warrior. The mastermind of important Allied victories in North Africa and Europe, Patton valued the support of his friend General Omar Bradley (Karl Malden in a quality supporting role). The drumbeat to replace the outspoken Patton is explored, as well as his anticipation of the Soviet threat to postwar Europe. This is the ultimate man's man war movie!

Most Memorable Man's Man Line: "No bastard ever won a war by dying for his country. He won it by making the other poor dumb bastard die for his country."—General George Patton (George C. Scott)

2. *From Here to Eternity* (1953. Dir. Fred Zinnemann. Cast: Burt Lancaster, Montgomery Clift, Deborah Kerr, Donna Reed, Frank Sinatra.) Although there have been several man's man movies dealing with the December 7, 1941, attack on Pearl Harbor (*In Harm's Way*, *Tora! Tora! Tora!*, and *Pearl Harbor*, among them), none has been quite as effective as this one. Oscar-winning director Fred Zinnemann really makes the audience care about the servicemen and their civilian girlfriends involved in that fateful event on the eve of America's entrance into World War II. Based on the novel by James Jones, this hard-hitting view of Army life in Hawaii just before December 7 received eight Academy Awards, including Best Picture.

Most Memorable Man's Man Line: "I'm just a private no-class dogface. The way most civilians look at that, that's two steps up from nothin'."—Pvt. Robert E. Lee "Prew" Prewitt (Montgomery Clift)

3. *Apocalypse Now* (1979. Dir. Francis Ford Coppola. Cast: Marlon Brando, Martin Sheen, Robert Duvall, Laurence Fishburne,

Dennis Hopper, Harrison Ford.) Filmmaker Francis Ford Coppola's stark vision of the Vietnam War with renegade free-wheeling Colonel Kurtz (Brando) at the center of the action operating from across the border in Cambodia makes for a one-of-a-kind man's man war movie. The reality of war is present in every scene. Highlights include a chilling ride upriver aboard an army patrol boat in enemy territory and a dawn raid on a Viet Cong–held costal village led by the demented Colonel Kilgore (Duvall).

Most Memorable Man's Man Line: "I love the smell of napalm in the morning."—Colonel Kilgore (Robert Duvall)

4. *All Quiet on the Western Front* (1930. Dir. Lewis Milestone. Cast: Louis Wolheim, Lew Ayres, John Wray, Arnold Lucy, Ben Alexander.) Recognized as one of the greatest anti-war movies, its theme of German school pals marching off to the horrors of World War I only to be maimed and killed one by one was way ahead of its time in its extreme realism. Director Lewis Milestone showed a view of war never before been seen on screen. This was before the days of computer generated images, so he cast 2,000 extras for the battle scenes. The movie grabs you from the get-go by showing the grimness of war through the eyes of a twenty-one-year-old recruit (Ayres).

Most Memorable Man's Man Line: "I'll take the mother's milk out of you. I'll make you hard-boiled. I'll make soldiers out of you or kill you."—Officer Himmelstoss (John Wray)

5. *Platoon* (1986. Dir. Oliver Stone. Cast: Tom Berenger, Willem Dafoe, Charlie Sheen, Forest Whitaker.) Oliver Stone wrote and directed this film, reportedly based on his own personal experiences as an American soldier in Vietnam. There's solid man's man ensemble acting, showing the variety of people who make up the fighting force. The audience clearly sees the soldiers' fears, weaknesses, and motivations all framed within the painstakingly detailed horrors of the Vietnam War. Stone, himself, is even seen on-screen in a small role, just as he was in several other of his movies like *Wall Street* and *Born on the Fourth of July*.

Most Memorable Man's Man Line: "He killed him, I know that he killed him, I saw his eyes when we came back in."—Chris Taylor (Charlie Sheen)

6. *Sands of Iwo Jima* (1949. Dir. Allan Dwan. Cast: John Wayne, John Agar, Adele Mara, Forrest Tucker.) Under the veteran directorial hand of Allan Dwan, this solid example of a man's man war movie follows a squad of rebellious Marine recuits from training in New Zealand in 1943 to the capture of Iwo Jima—acknowledged as one of the toughest campaigns of World War II. At forty-two, the star, John Wayne, was surrounded by bright young actors in their mid-twenties. Dwans's movie was so authentic that he cast the real-life Marines who actually raised the American flag after victory at Iwo Jima to do the same thing in this flick.

Most Memorable Man's man Line: "You idiot. When are you gonna wake up? You wanna see that dame again, keep your mind on your work."—Sgt. Stryker (John Wayne)

7. *Saving Private Ryan* (1998. Dir. Steven Spielberg. Cast: Tom Hanks, Matt Damon, Ed Burns, Tom Sizemore, Vin Diesel, Ted Danson.) Just when you thought you saw every meaningful movie about World War II, an extraordinary man's man moviemaker like Steven Spielberg comes along to present a war movie with a unique angle. Army Captain John Miller (Hanks) gets an unusual assignment and takes eight soldiers behind enemy lines to save Private Ryan (Damon). Ryan's the only surviving brother of four in his family to serve in the military. The opening scenes showing Omaha Beach on D-Day challenge anything ever filmed about this bloody World War II invasion.

Most Memorable Man's Man Line: "He better be worth it. He better go home and cure a disease, or invent a longer-lasting lightbulb."—Captain John Miller (Tom Hanks)

8. *Full Metal Jacket* (1987. Dir. Stanley Kubrick. Cast: Matthew Modine, Adam Baldwin, Vincent D'Onofrio, R. Lee Ermey.) This film focuses on an average guy and follows him through basic training to his work in the field as a Marine Corps photojournalist. It also covers the brutal fighting at the start of the Tet offensive of the Vietnam War. This two-hour-long motion picture delivers one of the most realistic Marine bootcamp portrayals ever to be put on a movie screen. Based on the novel written by Gustav Hasford, who also co-wrote the movie script with director Stanley Kubrick and Michael Herr, the film features powerful performances by Matthew Modine and Vincent D'Onofrio.

Most Memorable Man's Man Line: "Five-foot-nine, I didn't know they stacked shit that high."—Gunnery Sergeant Hartman (R. Lee Ermey)

9. *Born on the Fourth of July* (1989. Dir. Oliver Stone. Cast: Tom Cruise, Byran Larkin, Raymond J. Barry, Caroline Kava.) This film is based on the book by paralyzed Vietnam war veteran Ron Kovic. After feeling betrayed by the United States, Kovic became an antiwar and pro–human rights activist. This is a movie that focuses more on the aftereffects of war than the war itself—an interesting point of view. Oliver Stone shoots the film beautifully with the help of his great cinematographer Robert Richardson.

Most Memorable Man's Man Line: "Sometimes, Stevie, I think people, they know you're back from Vietnam, and their face changes: the eyes, the voice, the way they look at you, you know?"—Ron Kovic (Tom Cruise)

10. *The Thin Red Line* (1998. Dir. Terrence Malick. Cast: Sean Penn, James Caviezel, Adrien Brody, George Clooney, John Cusack, Woody Harrelson.) This second treatment of the story of a rifle company battling to win at Guadalcanal in the World War II Pacific Front has the edge over its predecessor (first done in 1964). While the relationship between Penn and Caviezel takes center stage in maverick man's man director Terrence Malick's later version, it's also the approach of going from soldier to soldier and getting into each guy's head that provides the overall strength of this film.

Most Memorable Man's Man Line: "I might be your best friend, and you don't even know it."—First Sgt. Edward Welsh (Sean Penn)

Chick Flicks

(I don't think so.)

**Smoking Cigars
Like a Man's Man**

They call cigars "the smoke of kings." From the $5,000 humidor that sits on your desk to the $1,000 lighter you keep in your pocket to your $200 cutter, cigars are a true lifestyle. There's nothing like when a man's man opens his humidor, looks at his selection, and picks his smoke. After that, he properly cuts and lights it. Finally, he sits back and enjoys the cigar—the most important step. Whether he's by himself after dinner, in his backyard, or with friends sharing a scotch at a fancy cigar bar, it's always an exciting experience.

As a musician, you always hear about music being a universal language, and I believe that's true. However, I believe it's also the same with cigars. You can get a bunch of different men's men together who don't know each other and are from different backgrounds and professions, throw some cigars into the mix, and suddenly they're old friends. It doesn't matter how much money you make, what kind of clothes you wear, or what kind of car you drive. What matters is that you all share a passion for cigars, and that you're sharing that *same* passion at that *same* moment. You can talk about baseball, golf, politics, women, or work, but underneath it all, those things are totally irrelevant—it's about sharing a passion for cigars. I've been in cigar stores where I've seen a multimillionaire CEO talking and smoking cigars with a bus driver. Talk about breaking down barriers! They were chatting away and puffing on their stogies with not a care in the world. Those two men's men probably would have never spoken or met if they didn't both love a good cigar. All of a sudden there's a camaraderie and a special bonding that occurs. That's what cigars do. They're a celebration of the "good life" that always brings people together.

Many men's men throughout history have been noted cigar smokers. General Ulysses S. Grant was possibly the biggest cigar smoker ever. Grant, who of course went on to become president for two terms, was the most photographed person of the nineteenth century and was known to smoke up to fifteen cigars a day. (By the way, that's not recommended.) Politicians like former President Bill Clinton really enjoy cigars during work and play (I won't even go there). Actors like Denzel Washington, John Travolta, Joe Pantoliano, and James Gandolfini are famous cigar aficionados, along with actor-turned-politician Arnold Schwarzenegger. Sports figures like Michael Jordan and Wayne Gretzky enjoy their stogies, too. Historical figures like Mark Twain and Sigmund Freud puffed on many back in the day. Also, comedians like the late Milton Berle and George Burns had a common love of quality cigars. In fact, in his older years, Burns once joked, "I smoke ten to fifteen cigars a day. At my age I have to hold on to something." They are all men's men who fully enjoy (or enjoyed) a good cigar.

Now, not every man's man smokes a cigar. Some do and some don't. Personally, I've always loved them. When I was growing up, my grandfather and father smoked cigars. As a young man, I smoked a cigar because I thought it made me look older and was the masculine thing to do. I eventually acquired a taste for them. I have even owned my own cigar line called Public Enemy (with my cigar mentor Lou Silver). It was a fantastic cigar, and anyone who smoked it loved it. There was a specific color we went after in the leaf of the tobacco. We also used a lot of secret ingredients, but if I told you what they were, I would have to put you in my trunk and give you a ride upstate. Also, the characters I've played on-screen have often smoked cigars. In films like *Gotti*, *This Thing of Ours*, and *She's the One* (where I played Jennifer Aniston's father) my characters were all cigar smokers.

Now, a cigar definitely helps add to your man's man character image, but only if you know how to smoke one correctly. A man's man can spot a rookie cigar smoker in a crowded room any night of the week. In this chapter, I am going to show you all the ropes to smoking a cigar like a man's man so you won't stand out in the crowd for the wrong reasons. You don't want to be that moron at the bachelor party who lights the wrong end of the cigar. Nothing is more embarrassing than having your friends (or more important, some hot exotic dancers) laughing in your face. If you want to look the man's man part, you have to learn to *be the part*. From selecting to cutting to lighting, I got you covered with the best cigar tips known to man. So, keep reading!

What to Smoke

Forty years ago, cigars were considered an elitist thing. However, that was before the cigar boom. Today, they're accessible to anyone. Back in the day, cigars were only for those men's men who could afford them, while today there are cigars within everybody's price range. For example, if you can't afford to smoke a $50 cigar you can still smoke a premium $3 cigar and enjoy and appreciate the experience just the same. Today, the cigar world is about what's new and what's different. In a man's man's cigar world, it's about what *you're* comfortable with.

Discretion is key when figuring out what cigar to smoke and what cigar is right for you. You need to select the appropriate cigar for the amount of time you have, because you do not want to relight a cigar. A man's man will never save a half-smoked cigar. Why? Basically, a chemical reaction happens when you're smoking a cigar; if you light it, put it out, and then relight later, it will never smoke or taste the same. If you do relight your cigar, you're not smoking the cigar the way that the professional blender intended you to smoke it. Let me put it this way: If you were making love with a beautiful woman and stopped in the middle of the throes of passion to go to 7-Eleven to get a Big Gulp, and then a half hour later tried to make love again, would you expect the sex to be as good? No. You would never stop in the first place. Same with cigars—you finish them to the very end.

When you're selecting a cigar, there are some important things to consider, and size is certainly one of them. A man's man will select the right ring gauge for him. Let me explain. If you are 4' 9", 120 pounds, a 50-ring gauge, 7½-inch cigar is probably not the right cigar for you aesthetically. If he truly enjoys a large cigar, a man's man won't give a damn and will smoke it anyway. But if you simply don't feel comfortable smoking a 7½-inch cigar, you're not any less of a man, either. In fact, you're more of a man for having the honesty to say that's not the right cigar for you.

Here are the various sizes a man's man can choose from:

The Sizes:

- Small Corona (3.9 inches)
- Half-cup (4 inches)
- Panetella (4.5 inches)
- Robusto (5 inches)
- Corona (5.5 inches)
- Corona Grande (6 inches)
- Pyramid/Torpedo (6.14 inches)
- Churchill (7 inches)
- Especial (7.5 inches)
- Double-Corona (8 inches)

When it comes to cigar smoking, a man's man doesn't care about price. A cigar does not need to cost a ton of money to be enjoyable. Men, it's all about the smoke. You can smoke a great $25 cigar and you can also smoke a great $9 cigar. You can like them both equally, but for very different reasons. A man's man will select the right cigar given all the factors—mood, time, flavor, etc.

It's all about what's right for the moment. Any real smoker will tell you that most of the cigars they smoke in 2006 are nothing like cigars of the same brand they smoked in 1995. However, there are some companies that never compromise on quality, even when the market is not doing well. For instance, a good quality brand like Davidoff is consistent. You can put thirty-two Davidoffs on a table and every single one of them will be identical—the color of the wrappers, the construction, the packing, and the smoke. That is what makes a good cigar, and that's what you pay for. Let me give you an analogy. If you ask for a Coca Cola on ice in a tall glass, you know what to expect. You already know what it's going to taste like, don't you? That's exactly what makes a good cigar. When you go to get your favorite cigar at a cigar store, you know what it's going to taste like. When you expect it to taste, burn, smoke, and last just as long as the cigar you had the last time and it doesn't, you get pissed! What makes Coca Cola such a success is the same thing that makes a cigar a success—*consistency*.

A lot of guys buy what cigar magazines tell them to buy. They can't make choices on their own. But a man's man makes a decision on his own. Now, you're probably saying to yourself, "Alright, what do you smoke, Frank?" Glad you asked. Here are my top five cigar choices, in the order that I enjoy them in:

FRANK VINCENT'S TOP FIVE MAN'S MAN CIGARS

1. Davidoff Double R (Dominican) ($25): This is the "Bentley" of cigars. It has quality, consistency, and status. You can smoke this cigar twenty years from now and it will smoke exactly the same as it smokes today. It has a mild, robust smoke. When a fellow man's man cigar smoker sees you smoking a Davidoff Double R, he'll know you are "in the know."

2. Padron Anniversario (size Diplomatico) (Nicaraguan) ($25–$30): This cigar is similar, qualitywise, to the Davidoff Double R. However, it's a much stronger smoke. This "kick you in the ass" kinda smoke is not for everyone, but if you like a strong cigar, look no further. It's sometimes hard to find because its release is limited by the company. So if you find it, buy all the cigars in the store!

3. Hoyo De Monteray (size Double Corona) (Cuban) ($25–$30): This is the finest Cuban cigar you can buy. It stands alone because of the taste of the tobacco from this region. It has consistency and quality. *Special note: Men's men buyers beware! Make sure you are purchasing a real Cuban.* How can you tell if it's a real Cuban? If it's too cheap, it's fake. You have to pay at least $500 for a box of Cubans. Also, if you're buying a Hoyo De Monteray in a restaurant, you could be paying up to $50 for this cigar, but believe me, it's well worth it.

4. Dunhill Gran Cru (#2 Torpedo) (Dominican) ($18–$20): In addition to the smoke of this cigar being excellent, its physical shape, texture and feel plays a big part in why a man's man wants to smoke it. It is a box-pressed square torpedo cigar. When you pick it up, the construction looks so perfect that you think it was rolled by a machine rather than a human.

5. Zino Veritas (Honduran) ($12): This cigar is affordable. It provides a similar quality and a similar smoking experience to, say, the Dunhill Grand Cru, without making you drop twice as much money on a more expensive cigar. At this price, I think the Zino Veritas is a great everyday cigar.

Why do I think the Davidoff Double R is the ultimate man's man cigar? First of all, it's large and demands time and attention to smoke. When you smoke a Davidoff Double R, you don't stand up and move around. You sit back and relax—certainly a man's man style. It's also a sophisticated cigar. You're not going to smoke a Davidoff Double R on your lunch break standing outside your office. Like I said before, a real man's man only smokes a cigar if he has the time to enjoy it. If you can enjoy a Double R in twenty minutes outside your office, well then, more power to you. The other thing about the Davidoff Double R is that I find it presents an interesting smoke blend. Now, people always talk about the "body of a smoke." In my opinion, body refers to its character. Body is the way the smoke feels in your mouth. So, you can have a very full-bodied cigar with a very mild taste—meaning that it's not aggressive or strong in taste, but can still be a very smooth, mellow, and full smoke. By that I mean the smoke actually feels heavy and it has depth and heft.

A Davidoff Double R is a 50-ring gauge, which allows the cigar to burn cool. You also have a lot of filler burning because of its thickness; you're going to get more smoke in your mouth, but you will also get more air in the smoke. At this length, the cigar changes phenomenally from start to finish. As you smoke, the tars, oils and everything else are moving through your cigar. Some of that stuff sticks in the filler leaves, so as you smoke the cigar down, you are smoking some of the residual stuff that has already moved through it. This allows the cigar to change. The Davidoff Double R is specifically blended so that there's a creaminess that never goes away. It's a versatile cigar. If you like a mellow cigar, I can guarantee you that it does not get too strong; on the other hand, if you normally smoke a very strong cigar, you will still appreciate the overall complexity of the Davidoff Double R and how it changes from start to finish. You can buy a Double R in New York, Las Vegas, London, or Hong Kong and it will still smoke the same. You will probably never smoke a cigar that has this much consistency year after year, cigar after cigar. That's why it's my number one choice as a man's man cigar.

Okay, I touched on some fairly expensive cigars in my top five list. The cigars I listed above might be everyday smokes for me, but they might not be an everyday smoke for others. That's okay. Don't feel that if you can't afford cigars like a Davidoff Double R or Hoyo De Monteray on a regular basis, then you shouldn't smoke at all. Smoke what you can afford and enjoy it! Everyone should find a "niche" cigar that they like. A niche cigar is what I consider a dispensable cigar.

What's the best place to buy a niche cigar? A small neighborhood tobacco store. When you're in a neighborhood that has a corner tobacco shop (or even better, if you're in a neighborhood where they might be rolling cigars), go in and make a point of *not* asking the counterperson for a specific brand. You should say, "I'd like the best hand-rolled cigar you have that does not have a band on it." I once bought a bundle of cigars in Miami that were hand-rolled and cost $88 bucks for 25 cigars. That's what I consider a niche cigar—a.k.a. "a throwaway." For example, you're on the golf course with some fellow men's men and you light up, take just a few puffs and then throw the cigar away. Maybe you smoke one-third of it. Who cares? It cost next to nothing, so who gives a damn? Every man's man has an everyday cigar he can rely on.

If cigars are a very important part of your life and you have just met a woman, then you need to let her know about your passion. You want a woman to love and appreciate you for you, and cigars are part of your personality. On the other hand, you also need to respect her and the way she'd like to be treated. Not sure what that's all about? Check this letter out . . .

Dear Frank,

I was on a dinner date with a girl I'd been seeing casually and the restaurant had an adjacent cigar bar. After dinner, I asked her to join me for a smoke. I don't think she'd ever smoked before. So, I was excited to take her "cigar-smoking virginity." When it came time to select our cigars, I was trying to impress her because I know that with women "size always matters," so I bought her the biggest, fattest cigar in the joint. We sat in some leather chairs and I quickly realized she had no clue what to do. I cut and lit her cigar for her and then lit my own. After a few puffs she started waving her hands like she was flagging in a 747 at Newark Airport. I'll admit there was more smoke in the room than a London fog, but hey, we were in a cigar bar, right? The date came to a screeching halt when she turned green. After ten unreturned phone calls, I'm getting the feeling this relationship's dead. What can I do better the next time?

Bob

* * *

Dear Cigar Un-Aficionado,

The first mistake you made was bringing a non-cigar-smoking woman into a cigar bar. You should have quizzed her during dinner to see if she was a cigar smoker or not. If cigars are your passion, then great. But they might not be your date's passion. If you are with a woman who's a non–cigar smoker, then bringing her to a cigar bar and blowing smoke in her face ain't cool. On the other hand, if you're with a woman who is interested in learning about cigars, then a man's man introduces her to them with dignity and respect. Cigar smoking virginity . . . WHAT!? Fattest cigar in the joint . . . EXCUSE ME!? *Show some respect, and genuinely help your lady explore her interest. My final advice is, take a cold shower, stop calling her, and lose my address.*

Frank

When it comes to picking a particular beverage to accompany a cigar, there are truly no rights or wrongs. If you like a particular drink and you like a particular cigar, and you like them together, then go for it, man. Who am I to say you're wrong? (Actually, if you're drinking a McFlurry from McDonald's with a cigar, I'm going to have to say you're definitely wrong!) Seriously, there are old-school classic options like cognac or port—drinks that have substance and body that will complement your cigar. Typically, back in the day, cigars were smoked by men after dinner. In England, after a big dinner meeting, they would present port and cigars to the attendees. That was a tradition, and still holds up in many countries today.

A man's man always selects his cigars first. Then, when it comes time to select a drink to complement the cigar, there are two ways to do it. You can match flavors or you can contrast flavors. So, if your cigar has a taste of woodiness and you want to match a drink to it, you would choose a scotch. That would complement the cigar nicely. If you're smoking a full-bodied cigar that has some richness and earthiness to it, you would match it with a single-malt, cognac, or dark rum. On the other hand, if you have a woody cigar and you want to contrast flavors, you would select something like a glass of champagne. You'll go from spicy, rich, leathery, and earthy in the cigar to bright, crisp, and clear with fruity flavors in the champagne. You're hitting completely different places on your palate. That's a fantastic way to contrast your taste experience, fellas!

Back to Basics

L et's review some basics and put them into a man's man perspective. In this section, I'm going to separate old cigar wives' tales, myths, and rituals from practicality. Hey, I know that I didn't invent the cutter or lighter. However, I can offer some generally accepted rules for smoking a man's man cigar. Let's go over the basics that set the stage for a man's man to properly light up. Just remember the three things that are always a must to thoroughly savor the art of cigar smoking: sit back, relax, and enjoy!

Cutting

A man's man does not bite the end of his cigar and spit it out like he's in some sawdust joint. He cuts it with a cutter. Now, he has two options for cutting a cigar: a closed cut or an open cut. A closed cut (commonly called a "punch cut" or a "V cut") removes a piece of the cap without removing the whole cap. I find that this can cause the cigar to burn unevenly or draw in a strange way. You see, when you smoke a cigar, the tars, oils and nicotines are moving through that cigar in the form of smoke. When you use a closed cut, those tars, oils and nicotines can get trapped in the cut as the smoke moves through. For that reason, an open cut (commonly called a "straight cut") is what I recommend. It removes the entire cap (the circumference of the cigar) so smoke moves through the cigar evenly—nothing gets trapped at the opening. Your cigar will smoke in a more balanced way, and most important, in the way it was intended to be smoked by the blender.

An open cut requires a guillotine-style cutter. A double guillotine is the ideal cutter, because it applies equal pressure to both sides of the cigar with the blades. With a single guillotine, you have only one blade coming down pressing against the bottom of the cutter, which can crush one side of the cigar. The single guillotine has to be razor-sharp in order to truly work correctly.

A true man's man takes it one step further, and uses cigar scissors to cut his stogie. Why? Well, because it's the most elegant approach, and it also gives you total control over your cut and angle. When you're using a cigar scissor, the cutting mechanism is out in front of you where you can fully size things up. Also, your fellow men's men can see exactly how much or how little you're cutting for them. The bottom line is that cigar scissors are just as effective as the double guillotine, but definitely more elegant.

Types of Lighters

Without a doubt, a man cannot accessorize like a woman can. For instance, a man cannot go out and buy a designer dress. (Actually, I guess he could, depending on what he likes to do on Friday nights.) However, a *man's man* has more limited options—cuff links, watch, tie, handkerchief, ring, etc. And, when it comes to cigar smoking, a lighter, cutter, and case.

There are basic rules when choosing what to light your cigar with. First, you do not want to use a "Zippo" lighter or other fluid-based lighter. Why? Because it's aromatic, which means that the aroma of the fuel has the potential to permeate the cigar. A man's man does not light his cigar with a scented candle, either. Unless you're hanging out with Madonna, keep the candle wax away from your stogie. An old-school way of lighting up is with a cedar match. Of course, cedar is aromatic and will undoubtedly permeate your cigar. However, many veteran cigar smokers feel that cedar enhances the way a cigar smokes and tastes. In the purist's mentality, which is how a man's man approaches cigar smoking, you want your stogie to taste how the cigar maker intended it to taste. If a cigar is boxed in a cedar box, then that blender intended the aroma of cedar to permeate the cigar. If the cigar is not boxed in cedar, then it wasn't supposed to be a part of the equation. Got it? Good!

Getting back to kinds of lighters: What lighter does a man's man buy? With all the choices out there in the marketplace today, this is not an easy decision to make. However, if you just bought a see-through lime green lighter at your local convenience store for under $2, I can assure you that you have just made the *wrong* decision. You want to purchase a lighter that does the job with precision and effectiveness, but also looks sleek and classy. For a man's man, I think the Davidoff Prestige ($400-plus) is the best lighter. It is manufactured by S.T. Dupont, which makes great quality lighters. Everything from the "ping" when you open it, to the solid feel, to the gorgeous lacquered and metallic finishes, makes this Davidoff lighter not only a highly presentable piece, but also a conversation piece. Most important, it has a dual flame, which is ideal for a cigar. Why? Because a dual flame is more wind-resistant and also gives you a wider flame. With a wider flame, you are covering more of the cigar's surface. Also, it's heavy enough that you know it is in your pocket at all times. Its impressive sturdiness and weight is a reflection of you. So, when you pass it to a fellow man's man, he says to himself, "Wow, now this is a lighter." Hey, you'd rather be overdressed than underdressed right? A man's man wants to have the best lighter in the room.

Lighting Up

After you have made your cut and unveiled your best lighter, you have to light your cigar. The way you light it is key. Real men's men use a simple and effective two-step procedure. The first step is to "toast the cigar," and I don't mean toasting it like an English muffin. Take the cigar and hold it out in front of you. Hold the flame of your lighter just below the bottom of your cigar. You want the flame to dance under the foot of the cigar—you do not want to put the flame directly on the cigar. Remember, you are just "toasting" it in this step, not actually lighting it. Then, when you see the tobacco start to glow, the second step is to put the cigar in your mouth. Begin to puff on it, and then fully light it by touching the flame directly to the end, rotating the cigar so that it is evenly lit. This two-step maneuver will guarantee proper ignition. Later, if your cigar begins to burn unevenly (referred to as "canoeing") only apply the flame to the less ignited portion until the cigar is burning on an even playing field. If you are engaged in stimulating conversation (like chatting with a gorgeous woman wearing a low-cut blouse), your cigar may briefly go out. Hey, it happens. If it does, repeat the simple two-step plan listed above and, most important, get the woman's phone number!

Here is a common question guys always ask me: *Is it better to light your fellow man's man cigar or to pass him a lighter and let him light it himself?* The answer is . . . both. There's honestly no right or wrong answer. The advantage to having someone light your cigar for you is that the other person can see the end. On the other hand, you know how you like your cigar lit. Also, if you opt not to light another fellow's cigar and pass him your lighter instead, you run the risk of "sticky fingers." (I've lost many lighters that way). My advice: A man's man passes the lighter already lit, or he lights his fellow man's man's cigar for him. Not hard, fellas.

Ashing

Ideally, you want to let your ash get as long as you're comfortable with (a longer ash allows the cigar to burn at its coolest). By the same token, if you're wearing a $4,000 suit, it ain't the time to have an ash contest with your Wall Street buddies, because you'll end up wearing it! A man's man ashes with care and class. Now, you do not tap your cigar on the edge of the ashtray to break off the ash. Instead, you roll the end of your cigar and allow the ash to fall off naturally. Remember, it's just a leaf—if you tap it too hard, you'll run the risk of cracking the leaf and, ultimately, the cigar will not burn properly. A man's man pays attention when he ashes, no matter how many cognacs he's had. Lastly, when you are through with your cigar, a man's man does not crush it into the ashtray like a cigarette. When you crush a cigar, it opens up the body. Then, all the tars and oils seep out and a disgusting odor will immediately invade your zone. The cigar just sits there cracked open, smoldering and stinking up the joint. It ain't a pretty scene. So, when a man's man is through with his cigar, he puts it down in the ashtray and lets it go out on its own.

Storing

Humidors can range anywhere from $500 to $30,000. If you are a man's man who takes cigar smoking seriously, you will definitely own one. If you haven't finished this book yet and are still in the "guy" category, let me put it into simple terms: Do you keep a twelve-pack of Bud in the trunk of your car for four weeks in August and then crack one open? No, because it'll taste like camel piss. So, you store the beer in a refrigerator. Okay, the same concept applies here, fellas.

Cutting

Toasting

Lighting

The most important characteristic of any humidor is that it seals properly, and that the humidification device turns on and off correctly. If you prefer to smoke a cigar either bone dry or soaking wet, I'm not going to tell you you're wrong. I'm just not going to smoke with you. Hey, to each his own. But, if you want to do it right, you need to maintain a precise balance of temperature and humidity that will keep the cigar in proper condition so it will burn, draw, and age properly.

The ideal levels are a temperature of 70 degrees and 70 percent humidity, but you can compensate. For example, if you can't get the room where your humidor is located to above 65 degrees, you may want to increase your humidity to 75 degrees in order to compensate for the lack of temperature. 70/70 ensures that the tobacco will burn at the proper rate of combustion, and that the filler portion of the tobacco will burn evenly in relation to the rest. It's not going to be so moist that you can't draw through the cigar because it collapses, and its not going to be so dry that the smoke burns hot. 70/70 will also ensure that when your cigars are in the humidor, the tobacco is aging properly.

You might have a humidor separated into top and bottom shelves, where the humidification device is only in the top lid. In that case, the cigars in the top of your humidor will be getting more humidity than the cigars on the bottom. So, how often do you rotate them? It depends. You take your hand and feel the cigars on the bottom and then feel the ones on the top. If it feels like the ones on the bottom of the tray are getting dry, then you've got to move them up. Remember, cigars demand the proper attention—certainly not hours and hours of time, but you do need to make yourself familiar with the process.

Once again, you do not want to add outside elements to your cigars—like cedar or other aromas that change how the cigars will age. In fact, cigars can affect other cigars in the same box. For instance, you do not want to put a flavored cigar in a humidor with non-flavored cigars. There is an aromatic component to that flavored cigar that can affect your other sticks. Also, if you just shaved and put aftershave on your face, you do not want to reach into your humidor and take out a cigar—they'll absorb all of that aftershave smell. In general, you want to keep what I call "naked cigars" (cigars out of cellophane) away from flavored naked cigars. Ideally, if you are buying cigars for long-term aging, then you should buy enough to be able to isolate those twenty or fifteen cigars in a humidor with a divider and let them age together, let the oils change within themselves without affecting your other cigars. Or, you should consider getting a humidor that will accommodate full boxes, and age your cigars in the boxes as they were intended by the manufacturer. A cabinet humidor is the best because it's electric and it accommodates full boxes. Of course, not everyone can afford that kind of equipment. If you are a normal man's man who owns one humidor and buys a few cigars a week, just rotate your cigars regularly to keep them fresh. The bottom line is to own a humidor of some kind and control the temperature accordingly.

Man's Man Cigar Manners

Okay fellas, here's some closing advice before you head into the big bad world of cigar smoking. Don't chew on the end of your cigar—that ain't cool. Nothing's more unattractive than a man holding a gnawed cigar, soaking wet from his own slobber, that looks like something his great-grandfather would have been smoking. Make sure you do not have tobacco on your teeth. Don't blow smoke in peoples' faces. Also, be careful of a 7½-inch cigar sticking out of your mouth when you are walking through crowds. When you turn to say hello to someone at a cocktail party, you could have a major problem! Lastly, a man's man fully respects the environment that he's in. I don't feel it is possible to enjoy a cigar knowing that there are people around who are annoyed that you're smoking it. If a man's man is sitting on a bench in Central Park next to a mother and baby in a stroller, he can't in good conscience enjoy his cigar. But, at the same time, expect a little bit of accommodation. For example, today in New York and Los Angeles you can only smoke at a few places—cigar bars and some outdoor cafés. Those are a man's man sanctuary to smoke, and if you're there, a man's man will thank you to keep your opinion to yourself! Listen, you don't have to be "Mr. Rogers" while you're puffing on your stogie, but just always remember to have some manners and class.

***

Man's Man Interview
with Vincent
"Big Pussy" Pastore

There is nothing like having a smoke with a good friend, and Vincent Pastore is definitely a good friend. I have known Vinny for over fifteen years, and he is a man's man through and through. During Vinny's movie and television career, he has played many unforgettable roles and worked alongside some of the top talent in the business. Who could forget him in his role of Salvatore "Big Pussy" Bonpensiero on HBO's hit series *The Sopranos*? Vinny has also had recurring roles on ABC-TV's *The Practice* and *One Life to Live*, as well as roles in major television movies like HBO's *Gotti* with Armand Assante and *A Slight Case of Murder* starring William H. Macy. On the big screen, Vinny recently appeared in *Revolver*, under the direction of Guy Ritchie. His other man's man feature film credits also include *Made* (John Favreau and Vince Vaughn); *Deuces Wild* (Matt Dillon); *The Hurricane* (Denzel Washington); *Serving Sara* (Matthew Perry and Elizabeth Hurley); and *Mickey Blue Eyes* (James Caan and Hugh Grant). He could be heard as the voice of "Luca" in the Dream-

Works animated hit movie *Shark Tale*. Also, if you're a man's man, you'll tune into the radio show he hosts every week on Sirius Satellite Radio called *The Wiseguy Show*. Vinny and I decided to talk over some high-quality stogies at the world-famous Davidoff cigar store on Madison Avenue in New York City. Check this out . . .

Frank Vincent: *Vin, I have seen many photos of you smoking cigars. What's the story behind that?*

Vincent Pastore: I started smoking on-screen when I first appeared on *The Sopranos* because my character, "Big Pussy," smoked a cigar. It was actually written into the script by David Chase. After that, I got very used to smoking them. What happened from the pilot of *The Sopranos* to maybe the second episode of season one was that I switched from smoking a big stogie on screen, to smoking little cigars. I made a choice for my character to smoke those small ones instead of the big ones because Jimmy Gandolfini was smoking the big ones all the time. I guess it was my way of differentiating "Big Pussy" from the rest of the other characters. Even in Guy Ritchie's film *Revolver*, Guy actually wrote my character smoking a cigar into the script.

FV: *We've known each other since the beginning of your career. How many movies have we done together?*

VP: The first movie we were both in together was *Street Hunter* starring John Leguizamo, back in 1990.

FV: *We were also in* **Witness to the Mob, Gotti, Under Hellgate Bridge, Remedy, This Thing of Ours** . . .

VP: We have been in a total of eleven movies together. Most recently, *A Tale Of Two Pizzas*, which I had a blast working with you on.

FV: *Me too, pal! Remember, we also did a play together called* East of Evil *by Philip Carlo.*

VP: Yup, Tony Sirico was in that, too!

FV: *In many of those movies I remember you smoking a cigar. Do you think it helps add to your character on-screen?*

VP: I think it definitely helps to define the character. There's a difference between a character in a film or TV show who's a cigar smoker and one who's a cigarette smoker. For instance, when I played Angelo in the movie *Gotti*, he chain-smoked cigarettes. By doing that, it showed his nervousness. However, when a character smokes a cigar, he appears a lot calmer, right, Frank?

FV: *More relaxed, absolutely.*

VP: As you know, there are scenes when you as the actor have to make the choices on whether to smoke the cigar or not. It depends what the scene calls for. Now when you're doing a play, there can be problems. I did a play recently called *Golden Boy*, with Maureen Van Zandt. Many people in the audience did not like the smell of the cigar I smoked onstage. It was a period piece set in the '30s and my character was a cigar smoker. So, I felt it was necessary. You have to play the moment onstage. Also, as an actor, you have to make sure you smoke the cigar correctly at all times.

FV: *So, a cigar has become part of your image, your style, per se.*

VP: Yes, the cigar defines a certain style for a character. For instance, you never see Tony Sirico smoking cigars on screen, but you will see Gandolfini or Joey Pants (Pantoliano) smoking them. It's just something you naturally adopt and then go with. Also, the type of cigar you're smoking can help define your character as well. When I was doing the hit mob comedy *Mickey Blue Eyes* (starring Hugh Grant and James Caan), Frank Pellegrino and I were on-screen partners and I came to the conclusion that our characters were "zips." Now, "zips" are guys who work in the mob, but are more lower-echelon members of the family. So, I smoked De Noble's.

FV: *Right, Al Pacino's character Sonny was like a "zip" in* **Donnie Brasco.**

VP: Yeah, yeah. More of a street guy. My take on it is that there are different levels of gangsters. So, if you were an upper-echelon gangster and had more money, you would buy yourself a $25 cigar, right?

FV: *Right, it's more to impress and look cooler. When you were growing up, did anyone smoke cigars in your family?*

VP: My grandfather Pastore smoked De Noble's. The old-timers smoked them, and they still do to this day!

FV: *During my youth, I was always intrigued by cigars. I thought they made you look grown up and like a man's man. As a kid, did you want to try a cigar when you saw your grandfather smoking one?*

Smoking Cigars Like a Man's Man 87

VP: Yes and no. Actually, I didn't start smoking cigars until my early forties, when I was working in nightclubs. When I worked the door at the clubs, I didn't like to smoke cigarettes. I liked smoking cigars because they lasted longer.

FV: *Vinny, just for some background, tell our readers about your history in the nightclub business.*

VP: I was in the nightclub business from 1967 till '87. They were places all located in Westchester, New York. The most significant establishments I worked

> **VINCENT PASTORE**
>
> **Favorite Man's Man Cigar:**
> Davidoff Double R
>
> **Favorite Character Played Who Smoked a Cigar:**
> "Big Pussy"
>
> **Favorite Legendary Man's Man Actor Who Smoked a Cigar:**
> Edward G. Robinson
>
> **Favorite Man's Man Drink to Have with a Cigar:**
> Remy or Courvoisier (with a water chaser)

at were the Lallipop and Peach Tree's, which was a big disco in New Rochelle, New York. I even owned a club called the Crazy Horse.

FV: *It was in the club business where you first got the acting bug, right?*

VP: Yes. It was from meeting actors Matt Dillon and his brother Kevin. They used to come to my club, the Crazy Horse, because they liked the rock 'n' roll bands that played there. They weren't into the disco scene. They were into the rock 'n' roll, shot, and beer bars. I used to overhear everyone bugging Matt to help get them acting work. I never asked Matt or Kevin for that kind of favor. However, after years went by and I decided I wanted to get out of the club business, I spoke to Matt and Kevin and they introduced me to their manager. I remember going to Kevin's manager, Charles Massey, at his office. I was literally in and out because I didn't even know what a monologue was. Then, I went home and I memorized a monologue and went back to see him.

FV: *Kevin Dillon is doing very well right now.*

VP: Yeah, he's on the hit HBO show *Entourage*. At that time, he had just done Oliver Stone's *Platoon* and he was hot.

FV: *Any famous men's men that you liked from cinema past who smoked cigars?*

VP: Edward G. Robinson in the movie *Key Largo* was definitely a man's man.

FV: *Big-time man's man.*

VP: Robinson even had the cigar in his mouth when he was sitting in the bathtub scene. He was the best!

FV: *Who are some famous men's men you have sat down and smoked cigars with?*

VP: James Gandolfini and I have smoked cigars together. I have also had the pleasure to have a smoke with actor William Forsythe. Actor/director/writer Jon Favreau and I smoked many cigars on the set of his film *Made*. I had a smoke with actor William H. Macy and our director from *A Slight Case of Murder*, Steven Schachter. But, one of the most memorable times was with Armand Assante, who loves to sit at a table with a bunch of men's men and just talk and smoke cigars.

FV: *Yes, Armand is definitely a great host. We had a great time at his house. Vinny, what do you like the most about cigars?*

VP: Cigars relax me. You can have a nice moment alone or with friends and just unwind. I like to smoke them more outside the house than inside. I live approximately 100 yards from the beach here on City Island, New York. Sometimes I light a cigar and walk to the beach. It is a great escape for me and helps me clear my head. To me, it's a form of meditation. There's nothing better in life than having a nice smoke.

**Mangia
Like a Man's Man**

The way to a man's man's heart is through his stomach. But that doesn't mean he's sitting around waiting for his woman to cook for him! Now, it's true that most "guys" don't cook, but a man's man can certainly hold his own in the kitchen. He lives by the motto "food is fun" and tries to eat and make different dishes all the time. A man's man *never* eats the same thing more than once a week. Hey, you go to the gym to work out, right? Well, a man's man works out his taste buds, too! To be a well-rounded, contemporary man in today's society, you have to know about good cuisine. You want to impress your woman, friends, relatives, colleagues—anyone you deem good enough to break bread with. I feel that breaking bread with people is one of the most personal and intimate things you can do, and a man's man *always* does it with style.

In all of the great mob movies that I've acted in—*Goodfellas, Gotti, Casino,* etc.—there's always a food scene. Those guys know how to *re-*

ally eat! There is a particularly great eating scene in *Goodfellas*. (Unfortunately, I spent this scene in a trunk.) It was when Tommy De Vito (Joe Pesci), Jimmy Conway (Robert De Niro), and Henry Hill (Ray Liotta) go to Tommy's mother's house in the middle of the night to pick up a shovel to bury my character, Billy Batts. They proceed to wake up Tommy's mother (Catherine Scorsese), and she then insists on making them a fresh Italian feast in the middle of the night. While they are eating you hear me banging from the inside of the trunk of the car. Could you believe those cold-blooded killers could relax and eat while there's a half-dead man in the trunk?

There's nothing like having friends over to your own home for a big meal. I'm going to show you how to do it with style. I think my passion for entertaining comes from my childhood. When I was growing up, we had great feasts on holidays, birthdays, and, of course, every Sunday! And a man's man respects traditions, and food and traditions go hand in hand. For instance, when I was a kid it wouldn't be Sunday if I didn't smell the mouthwatering aroma of my mother's delicious tomato sauce permeating the house, and Christmas wouldn't have been the same without roasted chestnuts at my aunt Jean's house! That's what food does for a man's man—it brings him back to the fondest memories of his childhood. I'm going to share with you a few of my mother's secret recipes that became traditions during my childhood. Be a man's man and make them with *your* family. But, there's an old saying, "God sent food and the devil sent cooks," so follow my cooking instructions to a T and you'll be fine. I'm also going to show you exactly what a man's man drinks. For example, there's nothing better than a martini before dinner. It enhances your appetite, and after just one, I guarantee you will enjoy your food better. From wine to scotch to vodka, I've got you covered with "top shelf" suggestions. If it ain't on the top shelf, fellas, then a man's man ain't drinking it. Remember that!

A man's man also appreciates good restaurants. Now, a good restaurant has top-notch cuisine, but it also has excellent service. It has to be the kind of place you wouldn't be embarrassed to take a guest. People tend to judge a man's taste on how good the food is at his favorite restaurant. Take them to some fugazi place, and they'll think you don't know the first thing about good cuisine. Here are some examples of what happens at a real man's man restaurant versus what you get at a fugazi one:

Man's Man Restaurant: You order a jumbo New York strip steak that feeds three.
Fugazi: You order a #3 and super-size it.

Man's Man Restaurant: The manager sends a round of Chivas Regal on the house.
Fugazi: The manager sends a round of Shirley Temples on the house.

Man's Man Restaurant: The valet takes your car.
Fugazi: The valet takes your car and then you realize there's no valet service.

Man's Man Restaurant: You put a 20 percent tip for your waiter on the table.
Fugazi: You put a 20 percent tip for your waiter in his g-string.

Now that we got that straight, let me take you on a tour of some of my favorite restaurants. The restaurants I list here are real man's man first-class establishments. If you can't make it to any of these places, don't worry! I've included some recipes, courtesy of these great places, for you to make in the comfort of your own home. If you do go to any of the restaurants I list in the next section, tell them that Frank Vincent sent you. Just be sure to tip the maître d'. If I find out you dropped my name without tipping, I'm gonna pay you a visit!

Man's Man Restaurants

Italian Stallions

PATSY'S

236 West 56th St., New York, NY (212) 247-3491, www.patsys.com

Still in the same location since 1944, the one and only Patsy's Italian Restaurant has been known for years as Frank Sinatra's favorite place to eat. A trip to New York City is not complete without a visit to this true man's man Italian restaurant about a block away from Carnegie Hall. Multitalented Chef Sal Scognamillo prepares signature dishes like succulent veal chops sicilliano, tender chicken contadina, and sirloin steak pizzaiola with peppers and mushrooms. I'm getting hungry just thinking about it!

IL CORTILE

125 Mulberry St., New York, NY (212) 226-6060, www.ilcortile.com
  Located in the heart of Little Italy, Il Cortile first opened its doors in 1975 by owner Carmine Esposito. Executive chef Michael De-Georgio (a graduate of the acclaimed Culinary Institute of America) serves creative classic Italian cuisine, which covers all the regions in Italy. The garden room in Il Cortile makes this one of the most unique dining experiences in all of New York. This restaurant is a favorite of my *Sopranos* castmate and friend Steve Schirripa.

GOODFELLAS

661 Midland Avenue, Garfield, New Jersey (973) 478-4000
www.goodfellasnj.com
  I think the name of this restaurant says it all! First opened in 1991, Goodfellas serves authentic Italian pasta, seafood, chicken, and veal dishes. They even offer a private room for all your special man's man occasions. The interior is beautifully designed by sisters Stacey Conte and Jamie Kreshpane. Award-winning chef Vincenzo Cardinale, straight from Italy, is considered the "Picasso of Pasta." Some of my recommended dishes are Linguini Frutti Di Mare, Polla Romantico, and Scaloppine Terra Mare. With incredible food, first-class service, and an elegant atmosphere, Goodfellas has all the ingredients for a memorable dining experience. Tell the wonderful hosts, Sam and Pam, and owners, Doctors Dan and Ken Conte, that you're a friend of mine!

RAO'S

455 E. 114th St., New York, NY (212) 722-6709, www.raos.com
  Rao's serves some of the best, if not the best, Italian food in New York City—only problem is getting a reservation. I think there's an opening for a table in 2020. But, if you can manage to get in, you will have a meal to remember. This East Harlem eatery (on the corner of

114th St. and Pleasant Avenue) has been around forever and is still a true family-owned and operated business. Owner Frank Pellegrino is not just a castmate of mine on *The Sopranos* (playing FBI agent Frank Cubitosi) but also a good friend. He's the consummate man's man host, always treating his customers with respect.

IL VAGABONDO

351 E. 62nd St., New York, NY (212) 832-8221, www.ilvagabondo.com
    Since it opened its doors in 1965, this Upper East Side eatery has become a second home to many New Yorkers. The open kitchen (the first of its kind) offers its patrons an inside look at how this Northern Italian gem operates. Go there hungry, because the portions are big enough for a king! Also, an indoor bocce court (free to all customers) solidifies Il Vagabondo as a unique man's man eating experience.

NORTHWEST

392 Columbus Avenue, New York, NY (212) 799-4530
www.northwestnyc.com.
    This Upper West Side eatery has first class ambiance and delicious food. The downstairs restaurant and sidewalk café (right across from the picturesque Museum of Natural History) is great for a power lunch or a dinner with friends. The upstairs lounge is the perfect romantic hideaway for you and a date. There are also great photos on display throughout the restaurant by legendary still photographer Brian Hamill. There are original shots of men's men such as Robert De Niro, John Lennon, Mick Jagger, Martin Scorsese, and yours truly. As far as the food is concerned, Bronx-born chef Gerald Zarcone is sixth generation Sicilian who started cooking when he was twelve years old. *Madone!* Try his rigatoni bolognese or the caprese salad (the buffalo mozzarella is flown in fresh from Campania, Italy, weekly). Northwest's owner, Matthew Paratore, keeps the restaurant's doors opened till some *real* man's man hours—two A.M. weeknights and four A.M. weekends.

LOMBARDI'S

32 Spring St., New York, NY (212) 941-7994
www.lombardispizza.com

There is a line out the door for a reason—you haven't eaten pizza until you've eaten Lombardi's pizza. Their secret: the freshest ingredients known to man and a 100-year-old coal-burning brick oven that gives the pies an unbeatable flavor. This restaurant is a must-visit because it's hands-down the oldest pizzeria in all of New York City (established in 1905). Their pepperoni and red onion pie is a favorite of Drea de Matteo. Hey, I'm having what she's having! Also, when you walk into the restaurant, there's a photo on the wall of neighborhood actor and my close friend Vinny Vella . . . you can't beat that!

NINO'S

1354 First Avenue, New York, NY (212) 988-0002
www.ninosnyc.com

This man's man list of Italian restaurants would not be complete without Nino's. *Elegance* is the best word to describe the décor and *delicious* is the best word to describe the food! I've been going here for years and have always had a first-class time. Their Grilled Red Snapper, Sautéed Jumbo Shrimp, and Penne with Braised Veal are must-haves. They also have a tasting menu ($60) consisting of Cold Lobster with Sturgeon Caviar, Wild Mushroom Napoleon, Alaskan King Crab and Capellini, Intermezzo of the Evening, Pan-Roasted Rack of Lamb Chop, Veal Loin Medallion, and Frozen Chocolate Cube. *Mama mia!* Men's men like Regis Philbin, Joe Torre, Stevie Wonder, not to mention supermodels like Cindy Crawford have all been spotted dining at Nino's. Supermodels and delicious Italian food—this is man's man's heaven on earth! With numerous other Nino establishments in Manhattan, including Nino's Positano and Nino's Tuscany, you're sure to leave New York City with a full stomach.

The French Connection

BALTHAZAR

80 Spring St., New York, NY (212) 965-1785, www.balthazarny.com

Beautiful food + beautiful people + beautiful décor = Balthazar. The red banquets, rustic mirrors and long wood bar are so authentically Parisian that when you look out the window you think you might see the Eiffel Tower! Go there with a man's man thirst, because they have a French wine list with over 300 bottles. Does a man's man eat crème brûlée for dessert? Yes, but only here, because Balthazar is out of this world! It's open late, but make a reservation because this place is busy at all hours. Also, you're in the heart of SoHo, so walk around to all the interesting shops before or after your meal.

LE GIGOT

18 Cornelia St., New York, NY (212) 627-3737

This little West Village French bistro with dim lighting and seating for only twenty-eight people makes it the ultimate man's man date restaurant. The only downfall is that they just have beer and wine, so load up on martinis beforehand. You have to try the lamb stew—incredible! As soon as you walk into Le Gigot, you get a warm, cozy feeling. But, you might not get a table, so be a man's man and make sure you call ahead of time. What I like most about this place is that it's not a tourist spot; it's filled with locals and people "in the know." So, do me a favor, don't tell anyone. *Capeesh?*

PASTIS

9 Ninth Avenue, New York, NY (212) 929-4844, www.pastisny.com

When you have a French bistro right in the heart of the meatpacking district, you know the Steak Frites is going to be fresh. If you have a craving for a Croque-Monsieur at an odd hour, it's not a problem because Pastis is open for breakfast, lunch, and dinner. I hope you don't mind A-list celebrities like Jude Law, Sarah Jessica Parker, and Bono sitting at the table next to you. Hey, if it's good enough for Bono, it's good enough for you. If a man's man is downtown and wants to splurge on some fine French cuisine, he needs to look no further.

LE JARDIN

1257 River Road, Edgewater, NJ (201) 224-9898
www.lejardinnj.com
   Overlooking the beautiful lights of New York City in nearby Edgewater, New Jersey (where they shot a movie I was in called *Cop Land*), this restaurant is just across the Hudson River from Manhattan. The elegant interior makes it great for a business meeting over lunch, although it's equally great for a romantic dinner date on the enclosed terrace or the outdoor garden. A taste of Paris in the Garden State—who would have thunk it?

Meat-etarian

MARKJOSEPH STEAKHOUSE

261 Water St., New York, NY (212) 277-0020
www.markjosephsteakhouse.com
   This Lower Manhattan Seaport steakhouse is "man's man 101." The house specialty, a mammoth porterhouse steak ($133, serves four), will make sure you never again ask the question, "Where's the beef?" The sides they offer, like mashed potatoes, creamed spinach, and sautéed mushrooms, are delicious, if you've still got the room. This is a favorite of fellow actor and close friend Tony "Paulie Walnuts" Sirico. Hey, I dare you to tell him you didn't like it.

SPARKS STEAKHOUSE

210 East 46th St., New York, NY (212) 687-4855

www.sparkssteakhouse.com

If you have always wanted to go to this legendary New York steak-house, but you're waiting to go on someone else's expense account, be a man's man and fire up the American Express! In fact, this is one of the most affordable high-quality steakhouses in the city. If you have good taste in wine, Sparks has got you covered. I am not sure what is better—the lamb chops, prime sirloin steak, or the service. It's unanimous among all men's men that the service at Sparks is remarkable, which can sometimes be equally as important as the food.

SMITH & WOLLENSKY

797 Third Avenue, New York, NY (212) 753-1530

www.smithandwollensky.com

If you're driving up Third Avenue in Manhattan, you cannot miss this small, two-level building with dark green–painted trim on sparkling white amongst the towering skyscrapers. Once you go inside, the turn-of-the-century design of wood paneling makes a man's man feel right at home. The "old school" waiters and menus in a wooden picture frame add to this "old New York" feel and dining experience. So, how's the steak? I think this quote about Smith & Wollensky from *The New York Times* says it all: "A steakhouse to end all arguments."

KEENS STEAKHOUSE

72 West 36th St., New York, NY (212) 947-3636, www.keens.com

Founded in 1885, Keens's ceilings are lined with over 90,000 clay pipes that were once owned and smoked by customers over dinner. They even have baseball legend Babe Ruth's original pipe displayed there. How about that for man's man atmosphere! I recommend sitting next to a fireplace, starting with a tomato and onion salad, and then having the Keens's legendary mutton chop as your main course. Their extensive list of scotch and wine is very impressive. If you're looking to host a private party, Keens Steakhouse can accommodate up to 400 men's men (or women!).

PETER LUGER

178 Broadway, Brooklyn, NY (718) 387-7400, www.peterluger.com

If you're a restaurant that's been open and packed every day since 1887, then you must be doing something right. In fact, Peter Luger has been proudly rated by *Zagat's* as New York's number one steakhouse for twenty years in a row. The owners have an in-house cellar where they age steaks at a top-secret temperature for a top-secret length of time. The result—a melt-in-your-mouth quality cut of meat. I think *Gourmet* magazine said it best: "Peter Luger maintains a level of steak quality that is simply unmatched in America." By the way, so you're not embarrassed in front of your fellow man's man guests when the check arrives: It's cash only, folks.

Eating with the Fishes

UMBERTO'S CLAM HOUSE

178 Mulberry St., New York, NY (212) 431-7545
www.umbertosclamhouse.com

Italian seafood specialties right in the heart of Little Italy—that's got a man's man meal written all over it! From when the restaurant opened in 1972, the owner, Umberto Ianniello, was opposed to serving anything other than seafood at his establishment, although around 1996, steaks and chops found their way onto the menu. But the star remains the clams and if you haven't eaten clams at Umberto's, then you really haven't eaten clams, period. This was where reputed mobster "Crazy" Joe Gallo was gunned down while eating the place's famous seafood.

Talk about indigestion! But, seriously, it is part of the history that makes New York's Little Italy a true "one-of-a-kind" colorful place.

BLUE WATER GRILL

31 Union Square West, New York, NY (212) 675-9500
This seafood restaurant right in the center of Union Square in Manhattan is a great spot. You can sit in the main room (quieter and good for a man's man power lunch) or in the jazz room (live music makes this room great for a dinner date). The selection on the menu (tuna, mahi mahi, salmon, swordfish, lobster) is quite impressive. I have to say, when I go there, I am never disappointed. The wait staff is friendly, attentive, and can answer any question you might have about their menu. Hey, seafood, jazz, and great service—now, that's what I call a man's man night on the town!

MARINA CAFÉ

154 Mansion Ave., Staten Island, NY (718) 967-3077
www.marinacafegrand.com
First opening its doors in 1980, the Marina Café has some fantastic seafood with great atmosphere, whether you're on a date or with a group of men's men. They have a fantastic raw bar with littleneck clams, bluepoint oysters, and chilled shrimp or lobster cocktail. Marina Café has a huge menu, so there is something to order for all tastes. The place even has a complete lobster dinner (Monday through Friday) for the price of only $21. My suggestion: Get a table on the deck overlooking Great Kills Harbor with a view of the beautiful boats that fill the marina.

OCEANA

55 East 54th St., New York, NY (212) 759-5941
www.oceanarestaurant.com

This man's man Midtown restaurant is centrally located (near Radio City Music Hall and the Museum of Modern Art) and one of the most popular restaurants in the whole city for seafood lovers. Executive chef Cornelius Gallagher makes you wonder how food can taste so damn good! The seafood tastes as if it was caught fresh that morning. With white-glove service and this prime location, Oceana is perfect for a lunch meeting or dinner with the lovely lady of your life.

✧ HOT SAUSAGES SAN GENNARO ✧

Patsy's

12 links (about 2½ lbs.) fresh hot Italian sausage
7 tablespoons olive oil
2 medium yellow onions, thinly sliced
1 14-ounce can Italian whole plum tomatoes, with juice
6 hot cherry peppers, seeded and sliced
1 teaspoon crushed red pepper flakes
Salt and freshly ground black pepper, to taste
2 tablespoons tomato paste (optional)
3 tablespoons chopped fresh basil
2 tablespoons chopped fresh flat-leaf parsley

Puncture the sausages in several places with a fork. Heat 3 tablespoons of the oil in a large nonstick skillet over low flame. Add the sausages and sauté, turning frequently to brown on all sides, until cooked through, about 15 to 18 minutes. Remove from the skillet and drain on paper towels. Discard oil from the skillet.

Heat the remaining 4 tablespoons of oil in the skillet over medium flame and sauté the onions for 3 to 4 minutes, or until onions are translucent and lightly golden. Coarsely chop the tomatoes. Add the tomatoes and juice to the skillet; bring to a boil. Reduce the heat to low, cover, and simmer for 25 minutes, stirring occasionally. Return the sausages to the sauce, add the cherry peppers and red pepper flakes, cover, and continue to simmer for 15 minutes, or until flavors have blended.

Season to taste with salt and pepper. Stir in the tomato paste (optional) and add the basil and parsley. Simmer uncovered for 2 minutes. Serve hot or cold.

*Note: for a mild recipe, substitute red bell pepper for the cherry peppers, do not add the crushed red pepper flakes, and use mild Italian sausage. ▪ (SERVES 4–6)

✦ ORECCHIETTE ALLO ZAFFERANO ✦

Goodfellas

2/3 cup dry white wine	*1/4 cup minced shallots*
1/4 teaspoon saffron threads	*1 1/2 cups heavy cream*
2 lbs. asparagus	*3/4 cup chicken stock*
2 tablespoons vegetable oil	*Salt and pepper, to taste*
1 lb. shrimp	
1 lb. orecchiette (ear-shaped pasta)	

Combine wine and saffron and let steep for 20 minutes. Cook asparagus in salted boiling water for 3 minutes then cut diagonally into 1-inch pieces. Heat oil in a skillet over medium heat and cook shrimp until pink, about 3 minutes. Transfer to a plate. Cook the pasta in salted water until "al dente," drain, and set aside.

In a skillet over medium heat, let wine-saffron mixture and shallots simmer for 3 minutes, before adding cream and chicken stock.

Reduce heat, cover, and let cook for about 7 minutes. Add asparagus, shrimp, and pasta and toss. ▪ (SERVES 4–6)

⤞ BRAISED SHORT RIBS ⤝

Balthazar

6 beef short ribs (5 to 7 lbs.)
2 sprigs rosemary
6 sprigs thyme
1 bay leaf
1 celery stalk, halved
3 teaspoons kosher salt
2 teaspoons coarsely ground black pepper
3 tablespoons vegetable oil
3 medium carrots, peeled and cut into 1-inch pieces
1 medium onion, roughly chopped
4 shallots, peeled and sliced 1/4-inch thick
5 cloves garlic, peeled and halved
3 tablespoons tomato paste
3 tablespoons all-purpose flour
1/2 cup ruby port
4 cups full-bodied red wine, such as cabernet sauvignon
6 cups veal stock (recipe below)

Preheat the oven to 325 degrees. Bind each rib with cotton kitchen twine. Place the rosemary, thyme, and bay leaf between the two celery halves and again bind with kitchen twine; set herb bundle aside. Season the short ribs with 2 teaspoons each of salt and pepper. Heat the oil in a large Dutch oven over a high flame until it smokes. In two batches, place the short ribs in the oil and brown well on both sides, about 3 minutes per side. Set browned ribs aside.

Drain all but 3 tablespoons of fat from the pot. Lower the flame to medium and add the carrots, onion, shallots, and garlic. Sauté for 5 minutes, or until the onion is soft and light brown. Stir in the tomato paste and cook for another 2 minutes. Add the flour and stir well to combine. Add the port, red wine, and the celery herb bundle. Raise the flame to high and cook until the liquid is reduced by a third, about 20 minutes.

Return the ribs to the pot (they will stack in two layers). Add the stock and the remaining 1 teaspoon of salt. If the stock doesn't cover the ribs by at least 1 inch, add water up to that level. Bring to a gentle simmer, cover, transfer to the preheated oven, and cook for 3 hours. Visit the pot occasionally and stir the ribs, bringing the ones on the bottom up to the top. They're done when the meat is fork-tender and falling off the bone.

Transfer the ribs to a large platter and remove the strings. Skim any fat from the surface of the sauce, and strain remaining liquid through a sieve into a medium saucepan. Discard the solid matter. Over medium heat, bring the strained sauce to a strong simmer; reduce the liquid until slightly less then half (4 cups) remains, about 1 hour. Return the ribs to the pot, simmer for 10 minutes to reheat, and serve. ▪ (SERVES 6)

→ VEAL STOCK ←

5 pounds veal bones
1/4 cup tomato paste
1 yellow onion, roughly chopped
2 large carrots, roughly chopped
1 celery stalk, including green leaves
1 head of garlic, halved horizontally

Preheat oven to 450 degrees. Heat a dry roasting pan in the preheated oven for 15 minutes. Add the bones to the hot pan and roast until they are well browned, about 1½ hours. Use tongs to turn and rotate the bones throughout cooking time. When the bones are well browned, add the tomato paste and chopped vegetables. Toss to combine, and continue roasting for an additional 30 minutes.

Transfer the contents of the roasting pan to a large stockpot and fill with water (about 8 quarts). Bring to a boil over high heat and skim off any foam that forms on the surface. Lower the heat to maintain a gentle simmer and cook for 5 to 6 hours, skimming fat from the surface every hour or so. Strain the stock through a fine-mesh sieve; discard bones and solid matter. Cool and refrigerate for up to 3 days, or freeze up to 1 month. ▪ (MAKES 1 QUART)

⇥ CALAMARI ⇤

MarkJoseph Steakhouse

3 lbs. fresh squid (tubes only)
2 teaspoons salt
2 teaspoons ground black pepper
8 garlic cloves, minced
2 cups cornmeal, 2 cups flour, blended
1 cup milk
Oil for frying

Clean and cut squid into small rings, then rinse in cold water. Pat dry (make sure to dry thoroughly). In a separate bowl, mix salt, pepper, and garlic. Mix squid with seasoning mixture, and let it sit in the refrigerator for 12 hours.

Dip squid in milk, and then coat with cornmeal and flour and shake the excess off. Heat the oil to 550 degrees. Fry calamari 2 to 3 minutes, or until golden brown. Serve immediately. ▪ (SERVES 4–6)

Your Mother's Always the Best Cook

Most of the important "life lessons" a man's man learns about giving, sharing, receiving and loving, he learns from his family—and the majority of the times, he learns them at the dinner table. When I was growing up, we had a home-cooked meal every evening, prepared and served wonderfully by my mother, Mary. Since my family didn't have a lot of money, we ate more peasant Italian food such as lentil soup, Italian chicken soup, escarole and beans, pasta, etc. Dinner would always be served with a healthy side dish, such as sautéed spinach or broccoli rabe. My mother prepared her delicious breaded veal cutlets once every two weeks, and they were always a special treat and a big hit (see "That's Entertaining" section for recipe). On holidays, my aunt Jean would make her fantastic eggplant. With the little money we had, my mother always made a fresh and delicious meal for her family—something a man's man respects deeply. Also, my father, being the man that he was, would make a point to be home to have dinner with his family every night without fail.

Then, of course, on Sunday afternoons we would have a big "Sunday dinner," the most important dinner of the week in an Italian-American household. We would go to church in the morning and when we got home my mother would start cooking. The anticipation would build as the aroma of her Italian "Sunday Sauce" filled the air. The sounds and smells of fresh basil, garlic, and onions being chopped were always present. Stewing in the Sunday sauce for hours would be braciole (stuffed with fresh Pecorino Romano cheese, garlic, and parsley), plump sausages, and meatballs (fried first and then de-greased on paper towels). I loved to dip fresh-baked Italian bread in the sauce and eat it. Then, for dessert (and especially on holidays) we would have delicious Italian pastries—cannoli, sfogliatelle, napoleons—you name it! Mmmmm, I'm starvin' over here!

My father was a man's man who took pride in helping my mother cook Sunday dinner. He was always striving to keep traditions alive. I remember a funny story from one Sunday dinner when I was sixteen years old. I brought a girl I was dating (not of Italian descent) to our house for our family feast. My brothers, my girlfriend, and I were sitting in the living room reading the newspaper and watching television while my father and mother were cooking up a storm in the kitchen. After a while, my father yelled, "Let's eat!" Then, when he got to the dining room, he told everyone where to sit and, of course, he would be at the head of the table. Well, my girlfriend stayed in the living room. This was maybe the second time my father met her, so he politely asked her to come in again. She said, "No, I'm not hungry." Let's just say that this girl "marched to a different drummer," so to speak. My father turned to me, totally pissed-off, and said, "What does she mean, she's not hungry? Tell her to come in here, now!" I managed to get her to come in, and she finally sat down at the dinner table. Then, my father proceeded to start dishing out the macaroni. Everybody got pasta, two meatballs, sauce, and so on. After my girl-

friend got her meatballs, she asked my father, "Do you have any mayonnaise?" My father looked at me and said, "You and her get out!"
My father was a real man's man and he didn't take any bullshit, especially at Sunday dinner. I know that Yankee legend Yogi Berra was famous for once saying, "It ain't over till it's over." But, if you're Italian
and your girlfriend wants mayo on her meatballs, it's definitely over!
To sum it all up . . . we never dated again.

Through the years, family structures and habits have changed.
For instance, Sunday dinner has almost become more rare than the
manatee. I'm not exactly sure why that is. But I'm convinced that it
will take a true man's man approach to bring the dinner tradition
back. My mother's recipes were handed down for three generations.
In fact, my mother taught my first wife, who was of Irish descent,
how to cook Italian. My children learned from her and right up
through this day, they make Sunday dinners for their families. Try
these recipes with your own family on Sundays, holidays, or any day!
Or, cook one with your wife. Just promise me you'll share these special Italian recipes with people you love. Oh, and one more thing:
whether you're Italian or not, please *don't ask for mayo!*

✧ MOTHER MARY'S LENTIL SOUP ✦

2 tablespoons olive oil

1 ham bone

*1 pound dry lentils, rinsed in cold water (remove all particles that
    don't look like lentils, because there may be some pebbles mixed in)*

2 quarts water

1 teaspoon garlic powder

1 teaspoon chopped Italian parsley

1 medium onion, diced

1 8-oz. can tomato puree

1 bay leaf
1 tablespoon salt
1 teaspoon ground fresh pepper

Pour olive oil into a large soup pot. Brown ham bone until golden on all sides. Pour 2 quarts of water into the pot and add the lentils. Bring to a boil. Lower flame and cook for one hour. Add garlic powder, parsley, onion, tomato puree, salt, and pepper. Bring to a boil; lower heat to low and let simmer for 30 minutes. Serve immediately.   ◼ (SERVES 4–6)

⇢ MOTHER MARY'S SUNDAY SAUCE ⇠

MEATBALLS
1 lb. chopped beef
1 lb. chopped veal
1 lb. chopped pork
1 cup Italian seasoned bread
  crumbs
1 clove garlic, finely chopped
2 teaspoons onion powder
1/2 cup Italian parsley, chopped

1/2 cup grated Parmesan cheese
2 eggs, beaten
2 tablespoons chopped basil
1 teaspoon salt
1 teaspoon freshly ground pepper
1/4 cup cold water
1/2 cup olive oil
1 lb. spare ribs
2 lbs. sweet sausage

In a large bowl, combine all the chopped meat. Add the bread crumbs, garlic, cheese, eggs, and herbs and spices and mix well, adding some water to keep the mixture moist. Roll the mixture into golf ball–size balls, or larger if you prefer. Put the olive oil in a 6-quart saucepot; turn the flame to high. When the oil is hot, lower flame to medium and fry the meatballs until golden brown. Place finished meatballs on paper towels and drain the excess oil. In the same pot, fry the spare ribs and the sausages until golden brown and place onto paper towels to drain excess oil.

(Note: the meat does not have to be cooked all the way. It will finish cooking in the sauce.)

SAUCE
4 cloves garlic, chopped
1 small onion, chopped
2 6-oz. cans tomato paste
3 28-oz. cans tomato puree or
    crushed tomatoes

1/2 cup fresh parsley, chopped
2 tablespoons salt
1 tablespoon freshly ground black
    pepper
1 tablespoon sugar
1 bay leaf

In the same sauce pot, sauté the garlic and onion until golden brown. Add the tomato paste and sauté for about 3 minutes. Add the tomato puree, fresh parsley, salt, pepper, sugar, and bay leaf. Return meatballs, sausage, and spare ribs to pot. Bring to a boil; then lower the flame and simmer for 2½ hours. The sauce can be used on any kind of pasta you enjoy. ▪ (SERVES 8)

✤ AUNT JEAN'S EGGPLANT ✤

2 eggs, beaten
1 teaspoon salt
1 teaspoon pepper
1½ cups plain breadcrumbs
3 tablespoons freshly grated Parmesan cheese
1 cup olive oil
1 medium-sized eggplant (peeled and sliced into 1/4-inch-thick
    rounds; should yield 12 slices)

Place beaten eggs into a bowl; add salt and ground black pepper. In another bowl, combine breadcrumbs and fresh grated parmesan cheese. Dip slices of eggplant into the eggs and then into the bread crumbs, one at a time.

Place olive oil in a 12-inch frying pan over medium heat. When oil is hot (test oil by putting one drop of water into the pan. If the water jumps up, the oil is ready). Fry eggplant slices for 3 minutes on each side or until golden brown. Place finished eggplant on paper towels to drain the excess oil. ▪ (SERVES 4–6)

✦ LAMB CHOPS A LA KATHY ✦
(Broiled with Honey and Lemon)
(Served with wild rice and mushrooms)

16 single lamb chops cut from the rib, about 1/2-inch thick
1 teaspoon freshly ground black pepper
6 tablespoons honey
3 tablespoons lemon juice
4 tablespoons soy sauce (low-sodium)
3 tablespoons crushed garlic

Sprinkle chops with black pepper and put into a large glass baking dish. In a separate bowl, combine the honey, lemon juice, soy sauce, and garlic, and mix well. Baste by spooning the mixture over the lamb chops until the chops are fully coated. Set your broiler to high and place lamb chops 4 to 5 inches away from the flame. Broil on one side for 3 minutes, and then turn them over and broil on the other side for 4 minutes to give you medium-rare lamb chops. Once cooked, remove from the broiler and let rest for 5 minutes before serving.

✦ BUTTERED WILD RICE WITH MUSHROOMS ✦

WILD RICE
2 cups wild rice
4 cups water
Salt and freshly ground black pepper, to taste
3 tablespoons butter

Place the rice, water, salt, pepper and 1 tablespoon of butter in the top of a double-boiler, or in a 2-quart soup pot. Cover and steam the rice for 1 hour. Fluff the rice with a fork and stir in the remaining butter.

SAUTÉED MUSHROOMS
1 tablespoon butter
16 ounces white mushrooms, quartered
3 tablespoons chopped Italian parsley
1 clove garlic, diced
$1/2$ small onion, chopped
Salt and freshly ground black pepper, to taste

Melt butter in a 9-inch sauté pan over low heat. Place onions and garlic in pan and sauté until the onions are translucent. Add mushrooms and sauté until slightly browned. Add parsley. Season with salt and pepper to taste. Mix mushrooms with the cooked rice and serve alongside lamb chops. ▪ (SERVES 4)

That's Entertaining

A man's man is a strong believer in the principle of "mi casa es su casa." In fact, he hosts dinner parties on a frequent basis because there's nothing like good friends combined with good food and drink. However, remember that being a good host is a lot like meeting a women—if you try too hard, they won't like you, but if you apply just the right amount of attention, you're sure to come out a winner. Here are my top five rules that a man's man must follow when planning a successful dinner party with his close friends:

TOP FIVE MAN'S MAN PARTY-HOSTING RULES

1. *Ultimate Fighting* should only be on Pay Per View—only invite guests who you know get along.

2. The words *beer run* aren't even in a man's man's vocabulary, so stock up prior to the event.

3. A man's man *never* yawns at his own shindig—triple espresso, pal!

4. If your friend's wife just got a new boob job, don't ogle them.

5. No matter how drunk you get, don't start a conga line (my aunt Jean did it all the time).

As the host, it's your job to make people feel comfortable and relaxed. Greet everyone with a smile, take their coats, get people a drink (pour a little heavy to make it a fun night). On this evening, there's no job that's beneath a man's man, so be on the lookout for spills to clean up, dishes to bus, and trash to take out. A man's man always makes his guests feel at home. Remember to spark conversation and have a few jokes in your arsenal if dull moments arise. Don't know any? I got you covered:

- *For Your Doctor Guests:* A friend of mine had skin trouble on his face. So he went to a dermatologist who gave him some female hormones. His face cleared up, but his CHEST broke out!

- *For Your Actor Guests:* Two talent agents are walking down the street. A beautiful woman passes by. One agent says, "Wow, would I like to screw her!" The other agent says, "Out of what?"

- *For Your Lawyer Guests:* A lawyer died and arrived at the Pearly Gates. To his dismay, there were hundreds of people ahead of him in line to see God. But, to his surprise, God left his post at the gate and traveled down the long line to where the lawyer was standing. Then God and one of his associates guided the lawyer to the front of the line into a plush chair right next to his desk. The lawyer said, "I appreciate all this attention, but what makes me so special?" God replied, "Well, I've added up all the hours that you billed your clients for, and by my math you must be 178 years old!"

For Your Italian Guests: What happened when a fifty-year-old consigliere had a sit-down with his ninety-year-old mob boss? He made him an offer he couldn't remember.

Setting the Stage

You want to be the host with the most at your party. Let me clue you in on some *serious steps* on how to set the stage for your event, as well as give you some recipes that'll have your guests begging you for seconds!

THE AMBIANCE

A man's man serves his guests cocktails and offers some snacks like crudités and a gourmet cheese selection. As far as how the dinner table should be set, a man's man goes by one motto: "Less is more." You do not need colorful tablecloths or fancy napkins. A man's man uses a basic white tablecloth and matching napkins of a pleasant fabric, and allows the colors of the meal to highlight the table. Lit candles (in votive holders) and flowers (reflecting the season) are essential, but make sure it is a low flower arrangement, because you do not want an overwhelming bouquet of flowers to obstruct eye contact between your guests. Put some fresh pre-sliced Italian bread on the table and in small bowl place some extra-virgin olive oil and a touch of freshly ground pepper, for your guests to dip their bread (more healthy than butter).

THE MUSIC

A man's man has music on throughout the evening. You should select background music that creates a tasteful ambiance and, most important, is nonintrusive. As your special guests arrive during the cocktail hour, you should play a touch of Brazillian bossanova music—classic tunes from Antonio Carlo Jobim, Joao Gilberto, with vocals by As-trud Gilberto and Stan Getz on sax. Tunes like "Corcovado," "One Note Samba," and the "Girl From Ipanema" are light and add a nice cushion of sound so your guests can speak to each other. Through the dinner hour, a man's man has on some early Frank Sinatra from his "Capitol years," including albums like *Here's That Rainy Day, Only the Lonely, Nice 'n' Easy* and others of that feeling. For dessert, I suggest playing the masterful Diana Krall and her album *The Look of Love*.

THE MENU

APPETIZER
Grilled jumbo shrimp served on sliced Italian bread
brushed with garlic and olive oil

Drink Served
Bellini

FIRST COURSE
Cavatelli pasta with sweet and hot Italian sausage
and shaved Parmesan. Served with slow-cooked fennel and mint.

Serve family style

SECOND COURSE
Mother Mary's fantastic breaded veal cutlets,
served with a side of broccoli rabe

Drink Served
Chianti Ruffino wine

THIRD COURSE
Fresh fruit and Italian pastries (only buy at your
closest Italian pastry shop, no fugazis allowed!)

Drink Served
Espresso and Sambuca

Recipes

APPETIZER

✦ GRILLED JUMBO SHRIMP ✦

MARINADE:
3 tablespoons extra-virgin olive oil
Juice of one whole lemon
6 basil leaves, chopped
1 tablespoon white vinegar
Salt and freshly ground black pepper, to taste
2 pounds of large or jumbo shrimp (11 to 15 shrimp to the pound),
    cleaned and deveined. (You will need 24 shrimp, three per person.)

Combine olive oil, lemon juice, chopped basil, white vinegar, salt, and pepper. Marinate shrimp in mixture for 20 minutes. Place shrimp on metal skewers and grill on high heat for 3 minutes; turn skewer over and grill for 1 minute on the other side.

✦ TOASTED BREAD ON THE GRILL ✦

1 loaf Italian bread, sliced into 16 pieces
2 whole garlic cloves
Extra-virgin olive oil
Assorted salad greens
Black olives, chopped

Rub bread slices with whole garlic cloves and drizzle olive oil on both sides. Place the bread on grill and toast for 30 seconds on each side. Arrange two slices of toasted bread on each plate, and place assorted salad greens on top of bread. Sprinkle chopped black olives over the greens. Then place 3 grilled shrimp on top of each slice of bread and drizzle with salad dressing.

DRESSING
1 teaspoon minced garlic
2 anchovies, chopped
Juice of 1 lemon
3 tablespoons extra-virgin olive oil
1 tablespoon chopped fresh oregano, or 1 teaspoon dried oregano
1 tablespoon chopped fresh parsley
1/2 teaspoon crushed red pepper flakes
3 tablespoons toasted pine nuts*

Mix ingredients in a bowl, drizzle over shrimp, and serve.
▪ (SERVES 8)

* To toast nuts: Cook in a dry pan over medium heat for 5 minutes.

FIRST COURSE

✢ CAVATELLI WITH ITALIAN SAUSAGE AND FENNEL ✦

1 1/2 lbs. cavatelli (cavatelli is a short curled noodle, available fresh, frozen, or dried; the dried noodles are shell-shaped with a slightly ruffled outside)
2 lbs. mixed sweet and hot Italian sausage
1 large bulb fennel, sliced thin
2 tablespoons extra-virgin olive oil

2 tablespoons fresh mint, chopped
3/4 pound grated Parmesan cheese

Put the sausages in a 9-inch skillet and fill the pan with water to the top of sausages. Bring the water to a boil, and parboil the sausages for 15 minutes. Remove from pan and run under cold water. Remove skin from sausages and slice into 1-inch pieces. Set sausage aside.

In a 3-quart pasta pot, bring 2½ quarts of water to a boil and mix 2 tablespoons of salt in the water. Place the cavatelli into the boiling water and cook until al dente, about 12 minutes. Drain pasta and set aside.

Slice fennel into ¼-inch slices. In a 16-inch sauté pan, mix olive oil and mint and bring to high heat. Place fennel into the pan and sauté until edges are golden brown. Add sausage slices and sauté for a few more minutes. Place pasta in pan and sauté, tossing to make sure it all gets mixed together. Season to taste with salt and pepper. Grate Parmesan cheese over top. Serve immediately. ▪ (SERVES 8)

SECOND COURSE

⟶ MOTHER MARY'S VEAL CUTLETS ⟵
(With a side of Broccoli Rabe)

16 veal cutlets
2 cups all-purpose flour
3 eggs, beaten
2 tablespoons cold water
1 cup Italian breadcrumbs
½ stick salted butter
1 cup extra-virgin olive oil
Sea salt and freshly ground black pepper, to taste
Lemon wedges

Pound the veal cutlets thin. Place flour in a medium-size bowl. In another medium-size bowl combine eggs and water and beat until mixed. Put breadcrumbs in a third medium-size bowl. Coat veal cutlets in the flour, and shake off excess. Then dip veal cutlets into the egg mixture and, lastly, into the Italian breadcrumbs.

In a large frying pan over high heat, heat the butter and olive oil. When the butter melts, lower the flame to medium. After a few minutes, place four cutlets at a time (or as many as will fit into the frying pan comfortably), and fry for 3 minutes on each side. Take the veal cutlets out of the pan and place them on paper towels to absorb the excess olive oil. Repeat with remaining cutlets. Serve with lemon. ■
(SERVES 8)

→ BROCCOLI RABE ←

1 bunch broccoli rabe
5 tablespoons extra-virgin olive oil
5 cloves garlic, sliced into thin pieces
1 teaspoon sea salt
1 cup water

Wash broccoli rabe in cold water three times, then slice at least 2 inches off of the bottom. In a pot, heat olive oil over high heat. Add the garlic and sea salt. When the sliced garlic is lightly toasted, reduce heat and let the oil cool down completely. After it does, add 1 cup water and bring to a boil. Add the broccoli rabe and leave on high heat for few minutes (or until broccoli rabe turns dark green). Reduce heat again and simmer for 15 minutes, or until broccoli rabe is tender. Drain and serve. ■ (SERVES 8)

Salud!

I think man's man inventor Benjamin Franklin said it best: "There can't be good living where there is not good drinking." A man's man is particular about what he drinks and the kind of glass he drinks it in. For instance, he does not order cocktails like Alabama slammers, red devils, or mai tais. His tastes are much more traditional—savoring a fine wine or a scotch aged to perfection. He doesn't drink fruity beverages and only uses an umbrella in the rain— never in his drink. Nor does he consume any alcoholic drinks from a blender. You'll see that in this section a man's man is *very* particular. Also I'll address dealing with bartenders and tipping them properly. Well, there's no time like the present. So, let's address it right now:

Dealing with Bartenders:

- A man's man is always prepared with his order.

- A man's man is always prepared with his money.

Nothing aggravates a bartender in a busy place more than some moron fumbling through his pockets and weeding through the lint to find a $20 bill. The bartender is standing there with a hundred other customers who want to order and, more important, give him or her a tip. A man's man always has his money ready. Also, he never snaps his fingers to get the bartender's attention. Hey, it's a bartender, not a basset hound. *Respect!*

Tipping

A man's man sets a precedent early in the night with a healthy tip to the bartender. For instance, if you're with a few friends and the bill is $40 on the first round, you will definitely be remembered by giving a $10 tip. You hand the bartender a $50 bill (if you have one) and say, "Keep the change." With a tip like that, you'll definitely get noticed next time around. If you give the bartender a $5 tip, that means you're an "okay guy." However, you won't stand out in the crowd when you want to order round number two. Although giving a $20 tip will be appreciated by your bartender, it's overdoing it a bit. By the way, leaving $1 will definitely *not* get you premium service. Hey, you're not checking your coat here, pal!

Quenching a Man's Man's Thirst

MARTINIS

You might want to order a martini just because you've seen James Bond order one. That's fine. But, a man's man does not walk into a bar and just say to the bartender, "I'll have a martini." You're going to look like a fool if you're not prepared for the question that follows— *"How do you want it?"* If you don't have the right answer, then your date or friends will know you're simply trying to pose. A man's man orders his martini in a very specific way. For instance, if you order a martini on the rocks, you'll notice your friends either laughing in your face or sprinting to the nearest exit. Ordering a martini on the rocks is equivalent to putting mayonnaise on a meatball (and you know how I feel about that). Also, if you don't specify what kind of liquor you want, you're going to wind up with the "well" shit, which is equivalent to rubbing alcohol. A man's man will specify his liquor every single time he orders. So, in summary, be prepared to answer the following questions.

Question: Do you want gin or vodka?
Translation: Old-school bartenders might not ask, because it's usually assumed that the name of the game is gin. But, if your bartender asks, a man's man drinks either one.

Question: What brand of vodka or gin?
Translation: Choose a top-shelf vodka—Grey Goose, Belvedere, Ketel One—or a top-shelf gin—Bombay Sapphire, Boodle, Tanqueray.

Question: How dry do you want your martini?
Translation: A very dry martini basically has no dry vermouth in it. A regular dry martini has a little dry vermouth in it, and so on.

Question: Do your want your martini "in and out?"
Translation: "In and out" means that the bartender pours the vermouth into the martini glass, swishes it around, and then throws it out. All that's left is the residue of the vermouth on the interior of the glass.

Question: Olive or a twist?
Translation: A man's man always orders three olives.

Question: Do you want it dirty?
Translation: Dirty means that they put some olive juice in your drink, not that they serve it in a lipstick-stained glass.

So, a man's man may order a martini as follows, "I'll have a dirty Goose martini, very dry, with three olives." See, martini ordering is very specific. I can't stress the point enough that if you just say to a bartender, "Let me get a martini," and you're not fully prepared, you'll have egg all over your face. *A man's man is always prepared.*

SCOTCH

After a big meal with your fellow men's men at a quality steakhouse, or even at your own home, it's great to light a cigar and have a top-notch scotch. There's nothing better. Many guys ask me if they should add water to their scotch. The whole point with a quality scotch is that it's so good and pure that you would never add too much water, because you really want to enjoy its true taste. But, you certainly can add a little H_2O. After you pour yourself a scotch, you should "nose it" and then taste it straight. Then, add a tiny splash of water, "nose it," and taste it again. If it tastes better than before, you can go from there. Truthfully, I very rarely drink a cask-strength scotch without a little water. If you're drinking something that's 120 proof, it's like throwing a lit match down your esophagus. So, put a little water in, but not a lot.

Now, you can either drink a single malt or a blended scotch. Remember, with a blended scotch you're looking for consistency; with a single malt, you are looking for adventure. A good single malt and a quality cigar is a match made in heaven. Here are some of my recommendations (with the year and price per bottle). Sip on some of these and you'll be drinking in style!

Single Malt

- Macallan 18 year ($100 plus)

- Laphroaig 10 year ($50)

- Ardbeg "Ugedail" Cask Strength 11 year ($90)

- Springbank 21 year ($100 plus)

Blend

- Pinch 15 year ($40)

- Johnny Walker Green Label 15 year ($50)

- Johnny Walker Blue Label ($190)

VINO

I have always loved wine. Fine wine, good food, close friends, and stimulating conversation is what a man's man lives for. Also, many medical studies have shown that moderate wine drinking can be very good for your health. However, in the world of the man's man, wine is strictly consumed at dinner. He does not drink wine in a nightclub/lounge environment. Women can walk around with wineglasses, but men cannot. A guy holding a wineglass at a bar just does not reflect sophistication or project a manly air. There is only one exception! At a wine and cheese party, where that's your only choice, you can walk around with a wineglass. Otherwise, wine is to be savored and sipped slowly in the comfort of your home or at your favorite restaurant.

When you open a bottle of wine, pour a glass, swirl it, smell it, and then immediately apply my three essential wine-tasting techniques:

STEP #1: The First Taste: Take a moderate sip from your glass of wine. This initial taste is when your tastebuds will first be introduced to the wine.

STEP #2: The Full Taste: Move the wine around in your mouth to get a real taste of it. You want to examine the body and texture of the wine, just like you would a beautiful woman.

STEP #3: The Aftertaste: Swallow your wine slowly and examine the taste that remains in your mouth. A smooth aftertaste that does not last too long is what you're looking for. If it is still there six hours later, then you're probably drinking Thunderbird. That's a no-no.

Here's my man's man wine list. I list some very nice bottles of red and white in moderate price ranges (ranging from $25 to $100). Listen, pal, if you don't want to spend at least $25 on a bottle of wine, you shouldn't even be reading this book. A man's man drinks quality stuff only—if you want to be a big dog, then don't play like a puppy. The wines listed below are not rare by any means. You can find them at your local wine/spirits store. Also, remember that a man's man drinks a variety of wines from different regions. Just one more tip: The appropriate temperature for wine storage at home is between 50 to 60 degrees Fahrenheit (with 55 to 60 percent humidity). Don't let your wine get above 70 degrees, fellas. You want your wine to age right.

Here are my man's man suggestions for red or white wine—whatever your tastebuds are in the mood for.

Pricing Chart

$ ($25–$45)
$$ ($50–$70)
$$$ ($75–$100)

Red

California

Jordan Cabernet Sauvignon 2001 ($$)
Larkin Cabernet Franc 2002 ($$$)
Neibaum Coppolla—Rubican 1997 ($$$)

Italy

Brunello Di Montalcino 1998 ($$)
Luce 2000 ($$$)
Bertani Amarone 1996 ($$$)
Angelo Gaja Barbaresco 1995 ($$$)

Australia

Laughing Jack Shiraz 2002 ($)

France

Chateau Pichon Lalande 1994 ($$)

White

Italy

Santa Margarita Pinot Grigio 2003 ($)
La Scolca Gavi Black Label 2003 ($$)
Livio Felluga 2003 ($)
Jermann Dreams 2003 ($$)

California

Ferrari-Carano Chardonnay Reserve 2002 ($)
Beringer Chardonnay Sbragia—Limited Release 2002 ($$)
Cakebread Sauvignon Blanc 2003 ($)

France

Louis Latour Corton-Charlemagne 2000 ($$$)
Domaine de Chevalier—Graves Blanc 2000 ($$$)

New Zealand

Cloudy Bay Sauvignon Blanc 2004 ($)

Quenching Your Lady's Thirst

It's essential to realize that if you're having a woman over to your place, you must know how to make drinks she enjoys. Don't forget, it's not all about *you*. The megahit HBO show *Sex and the City* really started the Cosmo craze, and it has become the drink of choice for almost all women. Even if they're not drinking Cosmos, women love drinks served in martini glasses. A martini glass is tall and it makes a woman feel elegant, classy, and sophisticated. *Here's a tip: If a woman runs her finger up and down the stem of the glass while talking to you, it's a clear sign she's interested in you.* Let me give you three standard drink recipes every man's man needs to know how to make for the lovely lady of his choice:

✧ COSMOPOLITAN ✧

3 ounces citron vodka (Absolut, Grey Goose, or Ketel One are all excellent choices)
$1/2$ ounce triple sec
$1/2$ ounce fresh lime juice
Cranberry juice, for color

Put all ingredients into a shaker with ice. Shake vigorously and strain into a martini glass. Garnish with a lime.

❖ APPLE MARTINI ❖

3 ounces of a quality vodka (not flavored)
1 ounce sour apple liquor or apple schnapps
Splash sour mix (optional)

Put all ingredients into a shaker with ice. Shake vigorously and strain into a martini glass. Garnish with a cherry.

❖ RASPBERRY MARTINI ❖

3 ounces quality raspberry vodka
1 ounce Chambord (top-shelf French liqueur)
Splash triple sec
Splash cranberry juice

Put all ingredients into a shaker with ice. Shake vigorously and strain into a martini glass. Garnish with a lime.

Listening to Music
Like a Man's Man

Music has been a major part of my life. It started when I was in grammar school, when I took piano and trumpet lessons. When I turned eighteen, I bought a used set of drums and went to work in a four-piece cover band called Bobbie Blue & the Arist-O-Cats. Gradually, we evolved into a six-piece group. During the day, I would do recording sessions with famous people like Don Costa, Paul Anka, Del Shannon, Trini Lopez and the Belmonts, and at night I would play in some of the hottest clubs in the New York–New Jersey area. I also produced and conducted recording sessions for my music mentor, Bill Ramal. Today, I'm still involved with the music business: I have appeared in many rap videos for world-famous hip-hop artists like Nas, Method Man, and DMX. That's a side of me I bet you didn't know!

When you think of a man's man singer, who comes to mind? Frank Sinatra, Ray Charles, Tony Bennett? If you thought of those per-formers, you're definitely warm, kid! But, to help you better understand music "my way" here's a list of man's man singers, and singers I'm not so sure about:

Man's Man Singer: Frank Sinatra—Do we have to explain why?
Not So Sure: Michael Jackson—Do we have to explain why?

Man's Man Singer: Elvis Presley—Rumor has it he had to put a restraining order out against female fans!
Not So Sure: Marilyn Manson—Rumor has it the Devil put a restraining order out against *him*!

Man's Man Singer: Tony Bennett—His music career has spanned six decades.
Not So Sure: Vanilla Ice—His music career spanned six weeks.

Man's Man Singer: Jerry Lee Lewis—He performs like a pit bull without a leash.
Not So Sure: Boy George—He performs like a poodle in a biker outfit.

I think from these examples you can see the type of performer that a man's man should be listening to. If the performer has female background singers, that's good, but if he sounds like a female, that ain't good. Also, it's not just the words he sings or instruments he plays, but the attitude he portrays on stage that's important.

Bottom line, a man's man has to have good taste in music. This section is the virtual sound track to a man's man's life. I will cover all the man's man singers like Sinatra, Springsteen, Presley, Jagger—even "honorable mentions" like Mozart! Hey, the wig might be a little suspect, but the man was a musical genius. I'm also going to cover the "do's" and "don'ts" for music when you're making love to your lady, drinking with your fellow men's men, and more. This section is guaranteed to be music to your ears! Hey, would I lie to you? Now, listen up—*literally!*

Top Man's Man
Music Legends

I n my experience, to say a person is a true legend in a certain field is to say that the person has combined a special quality of style and charisma with the utmost level of success. Success can wear many hats in the music industry—playing, writing, performing, producing, etc. I've had the good fortune of being in the music field for most of my life. My experience gave me the opportunity to meet and work with many unsung music legends. Common belief is that when a performer is very popular, he or she automatically jumps into the "legendary category." But, that's simply *not* true. There are many music legends that everyday people have never heard of. These are people who play in recording studios, concert orchestras, TV, and Broadway shows, etc. But that's a whole other list.

The music legends on my list are people who have reached the pinnacle of success and popularity, along with contributing something unique to society. That's what it's all about! Louis Armstrong was not only known for his music ability, but was also known as an ambassador of goodwill. He traveled all over the world and spread love and peace through the use of his personality and his trumpet. At that time in history, it wasn't an easy thing to do. Although his forte was comedy, Bob Hope was a song-and-dance man who brought many musical revues all over the world. He entertained our troops during World War II, the Korean War, Vietnam, Desert Storm, and other times when our troops needed moral support. He always said he was ready at any time to entertain our "guys and girls in uniform," especially at Christmastime. In fact, he didn't spend a Christmas at home for forty years.

A legend also touches his individual fans directly. Here's a true story: A friend of mine is a huge Bruce Springsteen fan. Last winter, he drove about an hour down to South Jersey to fill out a form to possibly win concert and backstage tickets to meet his idol, Bruce Springsteen. He got the form from the box office and went across the street to a bar to fill it out. The bar was packed, but he saw an open stool. To his surprise, the person sitting next to the open stool was "The Boss" himself. My friend said hello and told Springsteen what a big fan he was. They got into a lengthy conversation. Then, Springsteen asked him to write down his phone number. Sure enough, two days before the concert my friend got a call from Springsteen's road manager, saying there would be two tickets waiting for him at the will-call window on the day of the concert. Now that's a stand-up guy!

My list is filled with men's men who have made their mark in music, who reinvented themselves time and time again. They were and are stars on the stage of music and the stage of life. They're legends for all the *right* reasons. Let's take a journey through the man's man music hall of fame.

1. Frank Sinatra: The "chairman of the board" and leader of the legendary Rat Pack was undoubtedly the *ultimate* man's man entertainer—loyal to his friends, devoted to his family, and involved with his music right to the end of his life. Aside from being the late-night party guy who hung out at places like New York's Jilly's until the wee hours of the morning, the next day Frank could and *did* go into recording studios and deliver his songs like no other pop singer in the world. Just listen to his one-of-a-kind versions of "The Gal That Got Away," "One for My Baby" and "Only the Lonely," and you can hear the inner soul of a true man's man. On the other hand, listen to Sinatra having a blast as he swings with the Count Basie Band (Count Basic was also a man's man) to cool hits like "The Lady Is a Tramp," "You Make Me Feel So Young," and "Come Fly with Me." He also sang great hits about real man's man cities like New York ("New York, New York") and Chicago ("My Kind of Town"). I met Sinatra a couple of times in New York City at Jilly's bar. Ol' Blue Eyes was hands-down the most popular ladies' man of all time, scoring top honors for being with beautiful screen legends like Ava Gardner, Lauren Bacall, and Marilyn Monroe, just to name a few. This classic crooner was once asked about his many love affairs and Sinatra boldly said, "If I had as any many affairs as you give me credit for, I would now be speaking to you from a jar in the Harvard Medical School."

Most Memorable Man's Man Song: "My Way"

2. Dean Martin: The French movie sex siren Brigitte Bardot once proclaimed Dean's recording of "Sway" the song that turned her on the most. His romantic Italian songs like "That's Amoré" won girls' hearts over. He is truly my hero as far as being the personification of suaveness, coolness and presence, and it's easy to see why the ladies loved him. Dino would be the first to admit he didn't have the best voice in the business, but nobody looked like they had more fun doing it than he did. The man was charming and had a smooth-as-silk man's man style that's often imitated but will never be duplicated.

Most Memorable Man's Man Song: "You're Nobody Till Somebody Loves You"

3. Ray Charles: If you don't know who this man's man music legend is, then you should return this book and "Hit the Road, Jack!"

Born in the racially segregated south in 1930, Ray Charles endured much adversity because of the color of his skin. He rose high above all the negativity to succeed in a world and industry that constantly put him to the test. If you could give me about three months, I could tell you all of this man's man's hit songs, but here are a few to whet the appetite: "Georgia on My Mind," "Let the Good Times Roll," "I Can't Stop Loving You," "Crying Time," and more. Ray Charles is a real man's man because he didn't let his blindness ever handicap him. His legend continues to live on, thanks to the recent man's man Academy Award–winning performance by Jamie Foxx in the film *Ray*. Fellow man's man performer James Brown was once asked what set apart Ray Charles from his peers. "What set him apart? He was *Ray Charles!*"

Most Memorable Man's Man Song: "What I Say"

4. Tony Bennett: He may have "left his heart in San Francisco," but this man's man entertainer is still right here, pumping out hit after hit. Anthony Dominick Benedetto was born in 1926, in Astoria, Queens, to an Italian-born immigrant grocer. Discovered by legendary comedian Bob Hope at a Greenwich Village nightclub, he quickly assumed the stage name Tony Bennett (that Bob Hope gave him), and the rest is music history. With over 50 million records sold worldwide and ten Grammy awards on his mantel, this legend is the walking man's man sound track of standards in all of pop music. He's also the true renaissance man—an extremely accomplished painter as well as singer. I think this *New York Times* quote says it all: "Tony Bennett has not just bridged the generation gap, he has demolished it."

Most Memorable Man's Man Song: "I Left My Heart in San Francisco"

5. Miles Davis: If you look up "cool" in the dictionary, you might find a picture of Miles Davis. When the "Picasso of Jazz" plays one of his hit songs like "Now's the Time," "Bye Bye Blackbird" or "Blue in Green," it feels like you're not just listening to music, but connecting to Miles's soul. Known mostly for being a trumpet player, this man's man was also an incredible multitalented composer and bandleader. If we could all go back in time and sit in on a Miles Davis recording session we would all be better people for it. If you have a CD collection and you don't have Miles Davis's album "Kind of Blue," you ain't a man's man. So, run out and buy it and then we can continue this discussion.

Most Memorable Man's Man Song: "So What"

6. Elvis Presley: This "Hound Dog" is definitely the guru of the pelvic thrust, which made women go mad. With three Grammys and over 130 albums under his belt, this man's man entertainer is not just a legend but an icon. He was equally loved on-screen, appearing in popular movies like *Girls! Girls! Girls!* and *Viva Las Vegas.* "The King's" unfortunate death on August 16, 1977, rocketed him to man's man cult status. As far as Elvis sightings, yes, they have been reported. However, the next question should be, "Did you see him getting on or getting off the UFO?" *Thankyew, Thankyewverymuch.* Take it from me, Elvis has definitely *left the building.*

Most Memorable Man's Man Song: "Jailhouse Rock"

7. Louis Armstrong: To the world, he's known as "Satchmo," but to me, he's known as a man's man. Louis Armstrong was born in the rough Storyville section of New Orleans at the turn of the century, and became one of the foremost legends of jazz and popular music, both as a singer and a trumpet player. His gravelly singing voice was unique, and he perfected a relaxed vocal style that's widely known as "Scat." Armstrong's hit records of "Wonderful World" and "Hello Dolly!" are the highlights of his huge vocal output. When this man's man was asked if he minded comedians and musicians doing impersonations of him, Satchmo answered, "Not really. A lotta cats copy the *Mona Lisa,* but people still line up to see the original."

Most Memorable Man's Man Song: "Mack the Knife"

8. Mick Jagger: Music always took center stage in this man's man's career. Influenced by legends like Chuck Berry and blues master Muddy Waters, the Rolling Stones created a style that would change music forever. They performed hits like "Time Is on My Side," "Jumpin' Jack Flash," "Get Off of My Cloud," and too many more to mention. You gotta tip your hat to a guy who's sixty and still rocks with no shirt on in front of 60,000 screaming fans, mostly women. The Stones still put on one of the best live shows, and their loyal fans never leave disappointed. Jagger has had an equally successful solo career. On his album entitled *Goddess in the Doorway*, he has guest spots from men's men like Bono, Joe Perry, Rob Thomas, and more.

Most Memorable Man's Man Song: "Satisfaction"

9. James Brown: You are definitely a man's man if your nickname is "The Godfather of Soul." Brown started to show an interest in music at a young age, winning first prize at an amateur night contest at the ripe old age of eleven. After a rocky beginning, he became determined to make music his life. A true revolutionary in the music business, Brown created new styles including "funk" with his megahit "Papa's Got a Brand New Bag." He has the ultimate stage persona, showing off dance moves and footwork that defy gravity as he performs his hit songs like "Living in America" and "Sex Machine." By the way, we won't hold the way he looked in that mug shot against him.

Most Memorable Man's Man Song: "I Feel Good"

10. Bono: Unless you've been abducted by aliens, you have heard of Bono and the band U2. Actually, even if you've been abducted by aliens, I'm sure they've got a few songs of U2's on their intergalactic iPods. This Irish-born man's man singer, songwriter, sometime guitarist, and always U2 frontman has put out such popular albums as *Boy*, *October*, *War*, *Under a Blood Red Sky*, *Rattle & Hum*, and many more musical feats. I was even in a movie with Bono called *Entropy*. U2 has recently (and deservedly) been inducted into the prestigious Rock and Roll Hall of Fame. One very important characteristic of a man's man is a sense of humor, and Bono's definitely got a great one. In 2004, he received an honorary law degree from the University of Pennsylvania. His reaction was, "It really is an honor, but are you sure? All I can think of is the laws I've broken."

Most Memorable Man's Man Song: "Where the Streets Have No Name"

11. Bruce Springsteen: This man's man was not only "Born in the USA," he was born in my home state of New Jersey. His backup group, the E Street Band, consisting of Clarence Clemons, Steven Van Zandt, Danny Federici, Garry Tallent, Nils Lofgren, Patti Scialfa, and drummer Max Weinberg (one of the finest drummers around), is the best. Which one of Springsteen's albums do you think represents being a man's man, *Greetings from Asbury Park* (his very first effort in 1973), *Born in the USA* (one of the biggest-selling albums of all time), or *Born to Run* (which simultaneously landed Bruce on the covers of *Newsweek* and *Time*)? The answer: every album he *ever made!* "Streets of Philadephia," a song Springsteen wrote and sang for the major motion picture *Philadelphia* (1994) won him the Academy Award for Best Song.

Most Memorable Man's Man Song: "Born in the USA"

12. Steven Tyler: This man's man with a scarf on his microphone is definitely one of rock 'n' roll's all-time unique and charismatic ironmen. As the lead singer of Aerosmith, his career has spanned over twenty albums and over 100 million copies sold. His wild onstage presence has brought him fans around the globe; his wild off-stage antics with fellow bandmate Joe Perry made them both internationally infamous. In 2000, Aerosmith was awarded a star on the Hollywood Walk of Fame and in 2001 they were inducted into the Rock and Roll Hall of Fame. Recently, I introduced Aerosmith at a sold-out concert in Madison Square Garden. One thing's for sure, Tyler's world-famous lips have been a helipad for some of the most beautiful women in the world.

Most Memorable Man's Man Song: "Walk This Way"

13. Gene Krupa: When the so-called "ultimate dream summit" was held at Radio City Music Hall in the late 1970s, renowned drummers like Buddy Rich, Art Blakey, and Elvin Jones were in the forefront. But one drummer was missing—the great Gene Krupa. He was the guy who put drums as a popular instrument on the map. Unfortunately, Krupa had died a few years previously, in 1973. Krupa first achieved fame in the Benny Goodman Band. His amazing rhythm and lightning-fast reflexes put the spotlight on the drummer for the first time, and paved the way for other drummers who followed, including a young Italian-American kid from New Jersey—yours truly. Buddy Rich, Shelly Manne, Roy Haynes, Max Roach, and many other great drummers owe a debt to Gene Krupa. He was a true pioneer and a very special man's man drummer.

Most Memorable Man's Man Song: "Sing, Sing, Sing"

14. Stevie Wonder: "Isn't HE Lovely!" This man's man has been cooking up incredible music for decades. The "sorcerer of soul" throws in some funk, rock 'n' roll, jazz, and reggae, and the result is always a feast of great vibes and music. Blind almost since birth, Wonder was a child prodigy, learning to masterfully play the piano, drums, and harmonica all by the age of nine. After being signed to Motown for years, Wonder went out on his own and the results were top albums like *Talking Book*, *Innervisions*, and *Songs in the Key of Life*. I had the sincere pleasure of working with him on Spike Lee's film *Jungle Fever*. When you put on one of his masterful tunes, he becomes "the sunshine of our lives."

Most Memorable Man's Man Song: "Superstition"

15. Jerry Lee Lewis: You know someone is a man's man when a day is named after him. Well, that's the case here. Memphis, Tennessee, Governor Don Sunquist named April 28 "Jerry Lee Lewis Day." His performance of "Whole Lotta Shakin'" on *The Steve Allen Show* in 1957 opened America's eyes to a bright new rock 'n' roll star. In fact, many people think this man's man, who's nicknamed "The

Killer," invented rock 'n' roll. Lewis is often compared to fellow man's man entertainer Elvis Presley, but in my mind he's a true one-of-a-kind "wild man"! I think what Jerry Lee Lewis said about himself in a March 14, 1983, *Time* magazine article sums it all up: "I'm a rompin', stompin', piano-playing son of a bitch. A mean son of a bitch. But a great son of a bitch."

Most Memorable Man's Man Song: "Great Balls of Fire"

MAN'S MAN HONORABLE MUSIC MENTIONS

Billy Joel * Mozart * Joe Perry * Bobby Darin * Duke Ellington * Steven Van Zandt * Frankie Valli * Count Basie * Johnny Cash * Sammy Davis Jr. * Carlos Jobin

Music Picks

Music to Make Love By

Music and sex are like fire to a candle . . . you need one to light the other! During the throes of passion a *guy* has SportsCenter blaring in the background, while a man's man has the right music playing, which sets the appropriate mood for him and his lovely lady. You want to give your girl a night that she'll run and tell her friends about, because you know girls talk just as much as guys, if not more. That's right, there's no room for any "minute men" in this chapter. A man's man takes the time needed to get the job done. These love songs will make your evening with your lady a sweet symphony—one where you're the conductor orchestrating a night to remember. You also should have some added bonuses for your lady. For instance, if she's from Paris, surprise her with some French pastries. If she's from Milan, have a great bottle of Italian red on hand. If she's from Russia, keep a handgun under your pillow because they usually have a psycho ex-boyfriend from Brighton Beach they forgot to tell you about. Just kidding, fellas.

Listen up. If you put on the wrong love song, you'll find your lady putting on her clothes. If you put on the right song, in the morning she'll be putting maple syrup on your pancakes. Bottom line, if you don't set the right mood, you're setting yourself up for disaster. Break out the wine, scented candles, and massage oil, and get down to business with these tempestuous love tunes.

Top Ten Songs a Man's Man *Must* Play While Making Love

1. "Fly Me to the Moon" (Frank Sinatra): This list would not be complete without "The Chairman of the Board," or should I say, "The Chairman of the Bedroom"? If a man's man is having sex with a woman while listening to this song, he's not only going to fly her to the moon, he's going to give her a tour of the whole galaxy!

2. "Wicked Game" (Chris Isaak): If you saw this video (crowned MTV's Sexiest Video of All-Time) then we're already on the same page. Chris Isaak gets to roll around in the sand with half-naked supermodel Helena Christensen. Talk about a tough day at the office. Women love this song!

Most Memorable Man's Man Lyrics: "The world was on fire and no one could save me but you. It's strange what desire will make foolish people do."

3. "I Can't Get Enough of Your Love, Baby" (Barry White): This love song lets your lady know you're *definitely* interested in coming back for more!

4. "You Are So Beautiful" (Joe Cocker): Make sure you are

> ## FRANK VINCENT'S SPECIAL ADVICE
>
> A *guy* shows up to a woman's place with a twelve-pack of beer. A *man's man* shows up with a twelve-pack of condoms. Don't be a schnook—protect yourself.

looking at her and not yourself in the mirror when you're singing these words. Seriously, this is a great sensual song. In fact, it was playing in a great love scene in the man's man gangster movie *Carlito's Way* when Carlito (Al Pacino) and Gale (Penelope Anne Miller) are getting busy. *Ay caramba!*

5. **"Mrs. Robinson"** (Simon & Garfunkel): This is a song for a young guy about to cross over into manhood. Gotta love mature women!

6. **"Secret Garden"** (Bruce Springsteen): A love song that women go crazy for by "The Boss." This is a "win-win" for everyone! Who could forget the scene from *Jerry Maguire* when this hit song is playing and Renee Zellweger says, "You had me at hello . . . you had me at hello." That movie line makes women melt like ice cream in August.

7. **"How Deep Is Your Love"** (The Bee Gees): I know when you think of the Bee Gees you're thinking of some dudes with bell bottoms and more chest hair than a chimpanzee. But I assure you this song will get your lady (or ladies, if your having a career night) in the mood.

8. **"I Don't Want to Miss a Thing"** (Aerosmith): Since you "don't want to miss a thing," this song will be your segue to breaking out the video camera. Seriously, Aerosmith knows what women want and *all* women want this song!

Most Memorable Man's Man Lyrics: "Lying close to you, feeling your heart beating—And I'm wondering what you're dreaming—Wondering if it's me you're seeing."

9. **"Love Me Tender"** (Elvis Presley): You play this tender-loving hit, and I promise you that Elvis won't be the only one famous for the "pelvic thrust."

Most Memorable Man's Man Lyrics: "Love me tender—Love me true—All my dreams fulfilled—For my darlin' I love you."

10. "You Are the Sunshine of My Life" (Stevie Wonder): Let her know she's the "sunshine of your life," and in the morning you'll be seeing the sunshine come up together.

Five Songs a Man's Man *Never* Plays During Sex:

1. "Every Breath You Take" (The Police): Here are some of the lyrics: "Every breath you take—Every move you make—Every bond you break—Every step you take—I'll be watching you." If you play this song, the only police you'll see are the ones carrying badges and *your* restraining order.

2. "Why Don't We Get Drunk and Screw" (Jimmy Buffet): Wow, you're a regular "Don Juan De *Moron*" playin' this tasty love ballad.

3. "Celebration" (Kool and the Gang): If you haven't had sex since the Reagan administration, keep the celebration to yourself, sport.

4. "Centerfield" (John Fogerty): Check these lyrics out: "Oh, put me in coach, I'm ready to play today—Put me in coach I'm ready to play today—Look at me, I can be, centerfield." Okay I know they say you should think about baseball to enhance your sexual performance, but this is ridiculous!

5. "Hit the Road Jack" (Ray Charles): A woman's favorite pastime after sex is cuddling, so I think this title says it all. Also, if her name *is* Jack, you got a whole 'nother set of problems.

Music to Drive By

A man's man has a torrid love affair with his car and what's coming out of its speakers at all times! Whether you're driving in a rainstorm, snowstorm, dead of night, or the most beautiful day of the year, you need a song to go with the particular mood you're in. Whether you're going to work or to see a woman you love, a song can really pump you up. With this list of songs a four-hour drive will feel about as long as it takes to brush your teeth. While you're spanning the highways, you'll also be spanning the decades of the best man's man driving songs ever. This stellar list of music will make you want to call your buddies, gas up the SUV, and head to Vegas, baby! Take a cruise through my top man's man driving songs and I promise you won't be disappointed.

Top Ten Man's Man Driving Songs

1. "Route 66" (Nat King Cole): A man's man definitely "gets his kicks" when he's driving to this hit. This is the ultimate cross-country song.

Most Memorable Man's Man Lyrics: "Won't you get hip to this timely tip—When you make the California trip—Get your kicks on Route 66."

2. "America" (Simon & Garfunkel): Great driving song because wherever you're cruising—New York, Massachusetts, Texas, Colorado—this song will cover all fifty states!

3. "No Particular Place to Go" (Chuck Berry): Great man's man driving song if you're going nowhere in particular.

Most Memorable Man's Man Lyrics: "Ridin' along in my automobile—My baby beside me at the wheel—I stole a kiss at the turn of a mile—My curiosity runnin' wild."

4. **"Go Your Own Way"** (Fleetwood Mac): This tune is great to play if you're lost and arguing with your girlfriend over directions. Just pull over, open the passenger-side door, and the title of this song says the rest!

5. **"I Still Haven't Found What I'm Looking For"** (U2): Another great song if you're lost!

6. **"Girls, Girls, Girls"** (Mötley Crüe): Yup, that's what's on our mind's the majority of our waking hours. This hit song will definitely pump up you and your pals when you're driving to the club for a wild night. Hey, Mötley Crüe drummer Tommy Lee was married to Heather Locklear *and* Pamela Anderson. That's man's man 101!

7. **"Highway Star"** (Deep Purple): If you got a need for speed, this is your song.

Man's Man Most Memorable Lyrics: "Oh nobody gonna take my car—I'm gonna race it to the ground—Nobody gonna beat my car—It's gonna break the speed of sound." That's fast!

8. **"No Sleep Till Brooklyn"** (Beastie Boys): If the coffee ain't kickin' in, open the windows all the way and blast this song until you reach Bay Ridge.

Most Memorable Man's Man Lyrics: "No sleep till Brooklyn—Foot on the pedal—Never never false metal—Engine running hotter than a boiling kettle."

9. **"Crosstown Traffic"** (Jimi Hendrix): If you're stuck in some crosstown traffic, throw on this song to deal with the stress, because nothing's better than Jimi!

FRANK VINCENT'S SPECIAL ADVICE:

A man's man *always* gets his oil changed every 3,000 miles. Trust me, none of these songs are good while you're waiting for AAA on the side of the road.

10. "Pink Cadillac" (Aretha Franklin): Now, this is a song that would definitely make some older men's men proud. It was also from a movie I appeared in called *Wise Guys* (starring Danny DeVito and Joe Piscopo).

Man's Man Most Memorable Lyrics: "I love you for your pink Cadillac—Crushed velvet seats—Riding in the back—Oozing down the street—Waving to the girls—Feeling out of sight—Spending all my money—On a Saturday night."

Five Songs a Man's Man *Never* Listens to While Driving

1. "Easy Lover" (Phil Collins) Just because you met a girl at a bar and you're driving her back to your place for the night, you don't have to advertise it.

2. "Stayin' Alive" (Bee Gees): This song is only good if you make a wrong turn and you're lost in a "bad-ass" neighborhood.

3. "Freakin' You" (Jodeci): Too hot to play while driving with your lady—safer when you're parked with her in a secluded spot.

4. "I Can See for Miles" (The Who): Not if you're in a snow-storm, dummy!

5. "Highway to Hell" (AC/DC): Unless you got Ozzy Osbourne and Marilyn Manson in the backseat, this song ain't gonna click.

Music to Drink By

Can you imagine drinking without music? A man's man certainly can't. But this list of songs are not just good for St. Patrick's Day, they are good for every day. When alcohol, beautiful women, and men's men combine, someone is likely to be waving a glass in one hand and a bra in the other. Seriously, a man's man is as particular about music as he is about what he drinks. A man's man likes his drink served with a chaser of good music. These songs should be in the jukebox of your local watering hole.

Top Ten Man's Man Drinking Songs

1. "One for My Baby" (Frank Sinatra): Great song if it's "quarter to three and there's no one in the place except you and me." Sinatra was a man's man who wasn't afraid to knock back a few in his day, and he always did it with style.

Most Memorable Lyrics: "We're drinking, my friend—To the end of a brief episode—So make it one for my baby—And one more for the road."

2. "Scenes from an Italian Restaurant" (Billy Joel): This song works whether you're drinking "a bottle of red" or "a bottle of white." Suggestion? *Mangia* to this hit at Il Cortile in Little Italy.

3. "One Bourbon, One Scotch, One Beer" (George Thorogood & the Destroyers): I think this tune is self-explanatory.

4. "I Drink Alone" (George Thorogood & the Destroyers): This is a great drinking song if you just broke up with your girl, lost your job, or *if you just hate people in general*.

Most Memorable Man's Man Lyrics: "I drink alone, yeah— With nobody else—I drink alone, yeah—With nobody else—You know when I drink alone—I prefer to be by myself."

FRANK VINCENT'S SPECIAL ADVICE
Never forget to tip your bartender!

5. "Naked Women and Beer" (Hank Williams Jr.): This country western star cuts right to the chase, and I love it!

6. "Red, Red Wine" (UB40): Great song, especially if you're at Sparks Steakhouse (red is always better than white when having a steak).

7. "Whiskey River" (Willie Nelson): This is pretty much the only river you'll find a man's man rafting in.

Most Memorable Lyrics: "Whiskey River take my mind—Don't let her mem'ry torture me—Whiskey River don't run dry—You're all I got, take care of me."

8. "Free Fallin' " (Tom Petty): Tom Petty always serves up a good drinking song. But don't get too carried away and "free fall" off your bar stool, dummy.

9. "Tequila Sunrise" (The Eagles): You and your lady might see the sun come up with this song.

10. "99 Bottles of Beer on the Wall" (someone who was too drunk to copyright this): If you're still drinking and not lying on the floor when this song is over, then you're the *ultimate man's man*!

Five Songs a Man's Man *Never* Plays While Drinking

1. "Margaritaville" (Jimmy Buffett): Here are the lyrics: "But there's booze in the blender—And soon it will render—That frozen concoction that helps me hang on." If it was on the rocks, then you'd be on the "must-play list," Jimmy. A man's man *never* drinks anything out of a blender.

James Gandolfini and me on the set of *The Sopranos*

(Left to right) Uncle Jim, yours truly, and my father on my confirmation day

Mother Mary and her boy on my confirmation day

Yours truly and Mother Mary out on the town

A late dinner in the islands with my beautiful wife, Kathy

An up-and-coming man's man, my grandson T. J. De Franco

My first gig at
Stan's Bar in
Secaucus,
New Jersey

The Arist-O-Cats.
That's me on the
top right!

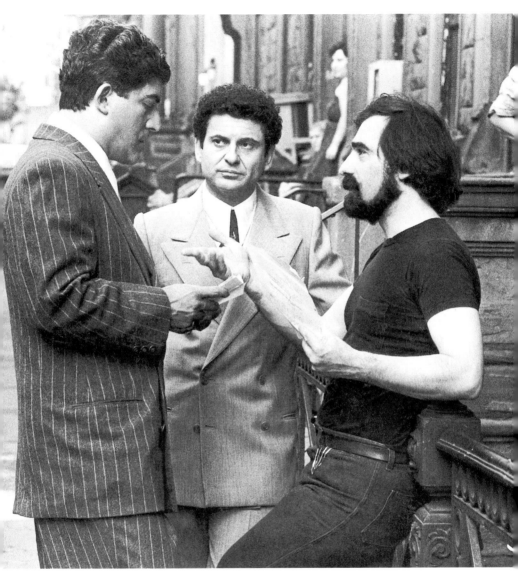
Rehearsing a scene from *Raging Bull* with Joe and Marty

Harmonizing with Dominic Chianese, aka Uncle Junior

(Left to right) Marty, me, and Joe on the set of *Casino* in Las Vegas

Puffin' away with my cigar mentor, Lou Silver

Diddy and me at the premiere of the movie *Belly*

Promoting my cigar "Public Enemy" in South Beach

2. "I Will Survive" (Gloria Gaynor): If you are listening to this song on the jukebox, my advice is to sober up for a second, look around, and make sure you are not the *only* guy in the bar.

3. "Roadhouse Blues" (The Doors): The key lyrics: "I woke up this morning and got myself a beer"! If you woke up this morning and the first thing you grabbed was a Corona; you don't need this song, pal, you need AA!

4. "Puff the Magic Dragon" (Peter, Paul and Mary): Hey, we're only drinking here, not getting the "munchies."

5. "YMCA" (The Village People): A bunch of dudes partying in a men's locker room dressed up as an Indian, cop, construction worker, and a biker—you do the man's man math!

* * *

Man's Man Interview
with
Steven Van Zandt

You may know man's man Steven Van Zandt from *The Sopranos* (he plays Silvio Dante) or as the longtime guitarist from Bruce Springsteen's E Street Band. But Steven is a true Renaissance man's man, writing and producing music as well! He is an acclaimed record producer for artists such as Bruce Springsteen and the E Street Band, Southside Johnny and the Asbury Jukes, Artists United Against Apartheid, Darlene Love, Lone Justice, Gary U.S. Bonds, Michael Monroe, Lords of the New Church, the Arc Angels, and many more top acts. A gifted songwriter, he has also written songs for artists including Jimmy Cliff, Southside Johnny, Gary U.S. Bonds, Brian Setzer, and Darlene Love. His material has been performed by artists as diverse as Jackson Browne, U2, Black Uhuru, and Eddie Vedder.

Now, being the coolest DJ in the country is just the latest chapter in Steven Van Zandt's long and distinguished musical career. His two-hour syndicated radio show, *Little Steven's Underground Garage*, continues to garner rave reviews. The program, which launched with twenty-three affiliates, has grown to an extraordinary 143 affiliates in 197 markets across the United States and Canada, and is only halfway through its third year. Additionally, the show is broadcast weekly on the Voice of America Music Mix Channel in forty-three different countries. Now those are what I call some man's man statistics! He's also an executive producer of *The Wiseguy Show*, a weekly talk show that features host Vincent Pastore. If there's anybody more qualified to answer some man's man music questions, I'd like to meet him.

Frank Vincent: *Who do you qualify as a man's man musician from yesteryear?*

Steven Van Zandt: You have to start with the original man's man himself, Frank Sinatra. I've just written a foreword to *Rolling Stone*'s new book, *The 500 Greatest Albums of All Time*. Even though *Rolling Stone* is a contemporary publication, in that foreword I talk about Frank Sinatra being the first man to do the "concept album." Sinatra made full use of the art form of the album because, as you know, growing up there was nothing but singles, and most of the albums of that era were best-selling compilations of singles. In 1955, Sinatra did a concept album called *In the Wee Small Hours of the Morning*. Very consciously and deliberately, he not only put together a coherent and consistent record, but also delivered a sequence of songs that told a story throughout. Sinatra was a true visionary.

FV: *And "The Chairman of the Board" did it on a two-track machine.*

SVZ: Yes, in those days they recorded like *real* men's men.

FV: *I recorded with Paul Anka and sixty men on a four-track machine.*

SVZ: There you go. There were no tricks or gimmicks in recording back then like they have today. Now, aside from Sinatra being the greatest singer of all time, everything he did became a classic and became his. I bet you half of the things he did were covers of hit songs before him that nobody remembers. But the reason why nobody remembers the original is because when Sinatra covered a song, he owned it.

STEVEN VAN ZANDT

Favorite Man's Man Band:
Bruce Springsteen and
The E Street Band

**Favorite Up-and-Coming
Man's Man Band:**
Boss Martians (out of Seattle)

**Favorite Man's Man
Album to Make Love to:**
Kinda Blue (Miles Davis)

**Favorite Man's Man
Song to Drink to:**
"One for My Baby" (Frank Sinatra)

**Favorite Man's Man
City to Perform In:**
Rome, Italy

FV: *You're absolutely right.*

SVZ: That was how distinctive Sinatra was as an artist. He is one of the very few craftsman you could call an artist. Technically, an artist is someone who writes his or her own stuff. As we know, Sinatra did not write his own stuff, but he came as close as you can come to that. When Sinatra sang a song, he communicated the emotion so clearly that it *was* like rewriting the song.

FV: *He probably inspired more singers than anyone in the world. Fine performers like Vic Damone, Tony Bennett, Bobby Darin, Dean Martin, and so many more all owe a debt to Sinatra.*

SVZ: Yes. First you look at Sinatra as an artist, but you also have to look at him as a human being and he was a force of nature. He was a leader and a visionary in everyday life, and his actions affected everyone. For instance, he took on racism full steam. Sinatra went to Las Vegas and made them let Sammy Davis Jr. stay in the same hotel as the white performers. That doesn't seem like a big deal now, but believe me, back then it was huge. Sinatra took on our entire society. Now, that's a man's man!

FV: *What about a man's man musician of today?*

SVZ: The equivalent to someone like Sinatra today would have to be a Bruce Springsteen. Bruce comes immediately to my mind. Now, I am not totally unbiased here, but I can also be objective to some degree. Bruce is another person who has never compromised in his own life. He didn't exactly fit in when he started out in music, but Bruce redefined what the mainstream was in approximately the same way Sinatra did. Bruce also broke racial barriers by having two black guys in the band. And, of course, he was a man's man by having Clarence right up front and making a statement. He not only had Clarence representing a multiracial band and communicating that type of brotherhood, but also having a saxophone in a modern rock band was a radical move, too! It was saying that we should not forget the past, because the sax was associated with the past and oldies. Every single record of the 1950s and the first half of the '60s, up until the Beatles, had a saxophone solo.

FV: *When I was playing, I always had a saxophone in my band. I had a piano quartet, but with a saxophone featured every single time.*

SVZ: Exactly. That's the way music was up until the Beatles. So, by Bruce putting Clarence in such a prominent position, he was saying that rock 'n' roll was a continuum. It's past, present, and future. There's a strong line of heritage going from the very beginning into the future and we should never forget that. Bruce did so many important things.

FV: *What originally influenced you to get into music?*

SVZ: For me, it was the "British Invasion," as they called it back then. It was the Beatles and the Rolling Stones. I've always been a band guy—I was not big on solo artists when I was younger. Later on, I grew to appreciate Sinatra, Elvis Presley, and the others. But as a kid, I just liked bands. The Beatles and the Rolling Stones changed everything because up until then, we had singing groups or instrumental groups or individuals like Chuck Berry, Bo Diddley, Little Richard, Buddy Holly, and people like that. There were no bands who wrote, sang, and played. There was no such thing. Technically, the Crickets was the first one and its leader, Buddy Holly, evolved out of that group very quickly and became more famous than the group itself. The Beatles really changed everything! Rock 'n' roll is really about bands, where pop music is about solo artists. Bands communicate friendship, brotherhood, and community, and that's what has always appealed to me. The Beatles broke the mold by playing their own instruments and writing their own songs. They played in places like Hamburg, Germany for twelve hours at a time, that's how they got so good. Not like today's wannabes who pretend they can play on MTV.

FV: *Bill Ramal, my musical mentor, started me as a studio player. Do you have a musical mentor?*

SVZ: I don't have just one mentor. There are certain ones I have for writing, singing, and guitar playing. As a guitar player, I would have to start with Eric Clapton. Clapton changed the entire nature of guitar in the modern world. I wrote an article about him for *Rolling Stone* magazine, pointing out that he was truly the one who made the guitar prominent in rock 'n' roll, as far as the lead guitar player goes. For a while, the lead guitar player was more important than the singer and that was because of Clapton. He took all the Black American blues guys and made their kind of stuff important. The English did a great service to us by giving us back our own music. The British Invasion of '64 and '65 was essentially a bunch of British guys listening to American rhythm and blues and interpreting it their way, and then giving it back to us in our own country. I didn't know who Chuck Berry or Bo Diddley were. These amazing British bands introduced us to them. As a guitar player, Eric Clapton really introduced us to our own heroes in American music.

FV: *"The Boss," Bruce Springsteen, is on my list of musical legends. How did you start working with him?*

SVZ: Ed Sullivan's CBS program aired on Sunday nights and it was the most watched television show of that era. Of course, now we watch *The Sopranos* instead. (Laughing). The Beatles played *The Ed Sullivan Show* and the next day, America went from no such thing as a band to everybody being in a band. Bands began rehearsing in their garages. (Hence the term *garage band*.) Now, even though everybody had a band, very few could make money doing it. Those of us who did, and there must have been eight or ten bands in our New Jersey Shore area, knew each other. Bruce came from Freehold and I came from Middletown, and we were on a circuit playing teenage clubs. It was a good time to grow up because there were a lot of places to play and be heard. We had beach clubs, high school dances, VFW halls, and teenage nightclubs. Bruce and I ran into each other a lot and became friendly. We played together in the late '60s and early '70s. Then, in 1972, Bruce finally landed a record deal. I joined the band for his third album, *Born to Run*. Basically, in those days, if you were in a band you became friends. In fact, if you had long hair, you were friends! There were so few freaks around back then that we gravitated to each other. (Laughing) That's how Bruce and I first became friends, in 1965 or so.

FV: *How does a man's man musician conduct himself on the road?*

SVZ: A man's man is someone who works hard, but also plays hard. So, you've got to give everything you've got onstage, but after the show, in the old days, if a beautiful girl wanted to show her appreciation, well, you took your inspiration wherever you could find it to keep you going.

FV: *(Laughing) Until the next town, right?*

SVZ: (Laughing) Of course, all that was before I got married. I've been happily married for twenty-four years. Now *that's* a real man's man!

FV: *A sign of a man's man is someone who keeps going no matter what the circumstances are. Did you ever have moments in your career where you had doubt and things didn't go as planned?*

SVZ: Every single day. Right now, I'm engaged in a revolution of trying to bring rock 'n' roll back. It's a fight every day. I woke up five years ago and realized there wasn't any new rock 'n' roll being played on the radio at all. The '50s music was being eliminated from the oldies stations and the '60s music was being eliminated from the classic rock stations. Also, there were no record companies signing any new rock 'n' roll bands. After thirty years of being in the mainstream, we disappeared. I put together a two-hour syndicated radio show, which we had to fight to get on. We fought to get on twenty stations and now, three years later, we're in 200 markets. I also have two channels we program on Sirius Satellite Radio. We're winning the war, but it's a battle because hip-hop, heavy metal, and pop music took over. I feel our children should have more choices, not less. So,

I decided to do something about it. Men's men don't stop and feel sorry for themselves. We just keep going, right, Frank?

FV: *Absolutely, Stevie! The sign of a man's man is someone who can reinvent himself. How did you make the transition from music to acting?*

SVZ: It was a matter of one phone call. David Chase phoned me and said he wanted me to be in his new television show. I said, "David, there are three problems. Number one, I'm not an actor. Number two, I don't want to be an actor. Number three, if I wanted to be an actor, why would I want to be on TV?" David replied, "No, I'm putting together a different kind of show, and I don't want to use the same faces everyone sees all the time." I told David to send the script. To be honest, I wasn't taking it very seriously. Anyway, I read the script and it was terrific! Then I got the part. At that point in my life, the mid '90s, I had walked away from music. I couldn't relate to it anymore—I felt it was time to do something else, but I had no idea what it was going to be. Destiny spoke! Once I got the part, I took it very seriously. I reread every single book written about gangsters. I also watched every gangster movie again. I found out where John Gotti got his clothes made. I did everything possible to create my character. I wrote a biography of my character, and discussed it with the writers on the show. I did everything I could do.

FV: *You had to believe yourself.*

SVZ: Yes, I had to look in the mirror and see somebody else. Being a musician my whole life, I knew who I was. But, this was different. I had to look completely different. I had to be unrecognizable physically to myself, and that would help me mentally be the part of Silvio. It really worked. I knew that when I walked out of that trailer, I would be acting with some very serious talent, like yourself. I wanted to hold up my end, and I wanted to live up to David Chase's faith in me.

FV: *You're a modern-day Renaissance man. You write, act, produce, sing, and play instruments. How do you do it all and do it so well?*

SVZ: I grew up in the '50 and '60s, which was a true renaissance period. I believe the '50s and '60s will be studied for years to come. The quality of the arts was so high back then that if you grew up during that period, you measure yourself by those standards. Whether it's Sinatra and those guys, or The Beatles and those guys, or the Brandos, Cagneys, and those guys, it sets a very high standard in your own mind. To tell you the truth, one of my biggest regrets in life is that I've had very little output. If you look at my whole life, I have had very little productivity. However, the upside is, when I finally get around to doing something, it is usually good. I guess somewhere along the line I decided if I have to choose, I'm going with quality over quantity. It takes a lot of time to do something right. A man's man says to himself, *If it's not great, then why bother doing it?*

FV: *Sounds like a man's man to me!*

SVZ: Frank, I wake up every day attempting to achieve greatness of some kind. Whether I make it or not, that's irrelevant. But, I fully intend to change the world every day.

Visiting Vegas
Like a Man's Man

L as Vegas is the ultimate vacation spot, one of the busiest destinations in the entire world. In 2005, approximately 40 million tourists visited the desert hotspot. This once barren desert was first developed by mob interests in the 1940s, but is now a land of corporate hotel resorts that are spending big time to show you a great time. Now, I consider Las Vegas to be the ultimate man's man destination. Why? Because of the gambling, entertainment, women, restaurants, clubs—all the things we *really* enjoy.

The women in Vegas are some of the most beautiful in the world. But, always make sure you are talking to the ones who are filing 1099s at the end of the year. How does a man's man know if he's talking to a woman and not a "woman of the night"? If you ask the woman you're talking to where she's staying and she says, "I'm staying at the MGM Grand for the weekend," you're safe. If you ask her where she's staying and she replies, "I'm staying at the Motel Grand for the next forty-five minutes," turn and quickly walk away. Also, a man's man

TOP FIVE MAN'S MAN VEGAS FLICKS

1. Casino: (1995; dir: Martin Scorsese; cast: Robert De Niro, Joe Pesci, Sharon Stone, Frank Vincent)

2. Bugsy (1991; dir: Barry Levinson; cast: Warren Beatty, Annette Bening, Harvey Keitel, Ben Kingsley)

3. Oceans 11 (1960; dir: Lewis Milestone; cast: Frank Sinatra, Dean Martin, Sammy Davis, Jr., Peter Lawford, Joey Bishop)

4. Leaving Las Vegas (1995; dir: Mike Figgis; cast: Nicolas Cage, Elisabeth Shue)

5. Oceans Eleven (2001; dir: Steven Soderbergh; cast: George Clooney, Julia Roberts, Andy Garcia, Brad Pitt, Matt Damon, Don Cheadle)

only hangs out at the current hot spots. For instance, you'll certainly find him playing blackjack at the Hard Rock Hotel Casino; however, you won't find him at the Liberace Museum. You see, a man's man spends his time in Sin City wisely. Vegas is like no other place in the world, and a man's man has to make sure that when he gets there he has a one-of-a-kind vacation!

I first went to Las Vegas in 1972. I went for pure pleasure, and I had a blast. Then, in 1994, I got a chance to go back to Vegas when Martin Scorsese cast me as Frankie Marino in *Casino*. When I got the script, I knew it was going to be a lot of fun. Why? Because we would be shooting in Las Vegas for four months straight! However, I also knew the film was going to be a lot of hard work. First of all, shooting a film in a casino is one of the most difficult feats in cinema. Being the man's man he is, Scorcese was definitely up to the challenge. It's certainly not easy to capture Vegas on film, but I think Scorsese did a masterful job. We shot nights at the famous Riviera Hotel. In fact, that's where I first met Steve Schirippa (Bobby Bacala from *The Sopranos*). At that time, Steve was the entertainment director of the Riviera. I have great memories from filming that movie. I think it's the number-one man's man film ever shot in Las Vegas.

While we were filming *Casino*, I definitely did some gambling during my off time. How could you not? In Vegas, there are slot machines in the supermarkets! I'm surprised they don't have slot machines in the bathroom stalls so you can play when you're sitting on the can. I *love* to play craps (no pun intended). The game has constant action. You can put yourself in for a thousand dollars, or even just a hundred dollars, and if someone hits a thirty-minute roll, you could pick yourself up a half a million dollars just like that! Once I was at a craps table in Vegas with two kids who had driven down from Northern California in their $50 car and gotten married. The young girl had just $5 on the pass line. Now, I am going to be dead honest with you—this girl shot the dice for an hour and forty-five minutes straight. She made one guy $250,000 and he threw her $10,000. Then, each of his buddies made some very good money as well, so they threw her $5,000. These kids made $40,000 on $5. What numbers! These kids had never seen so much money in their lives. You know what they said? "We're going to go home and buy ourselves a trailer!" That's what Vegas does, it makes dreams come true.

Another game I really love is blackjack. Now, when he's at the blackjack table, a man's man definitely plays with a system. He knows his strategy and makes each move correctly and without hesitation. When the right play is to double down, a man's man puts up his chips with confidence, never with trepidation. Even when a man's man loses, he still believes he did the right thing and has no regrets. He waits until the dealer has paid out every player and cleared all the cards before reaching for his chips or placing his next bet. So many people are overanxious and start grabbing for their money as soon as it's handed out. Calm down . . . it's not going anywhere. Here are some common blackjack questions that aspiring men's men ask me:

Question: Do you always split aces?
Man's Man Answer: You always split your aces (also your eights).

Question: How about splitting tens?
Man's Man Answer: You never splits your tens. If you had twenty-inches, would you cut it in half? I don't think so.

Question: Do you always stay on hard seventeen?
Man's Man Answer: The hard seventeen is often referred to as the mother-in-law hand—you want to hit it, but you can't.

Question: Do you ever surrender your hand?
Man's Man Answer: You should never be afraid to surrender your hand in certain situations. It may seem weak, but at the end of the day you'll keep more money in your pocket. For instance, you should surrender a fifteen against a dealer's ten, or a sixteen against a dealers nine, ten, or ace.

Question: What should you do when the dealer offers you insurance?
Man's Man Answer: Unless the dealer is offering Geico car insurance, don't take it. Statistically, it's a bad bet and a weak move.

Question: How about the "locust effect" of moving from table to table and spending no more than fifteen minutes at each table?
Man's Man Answer: I am not a fan of the locust effect. I think if a table is hot, you need to ride it as long as you can. If it's cold, you need to know when to walk away. Like the song says, "You got to know when to hold them and know when to fold them."

Okay, you've memorized all of my gambling tips before you left your house for a wild week in Sin City. You're descending into Las Vegas International Airport and from your window seat, you see the lights of the Strip gleaming in the dark of the night. Does it get any better than that? No way. Las Vegas is excitement personified. In this section, I am going to cover all your bases for a one-of-a-kind man's man trip to the city that celebrated its 100th birthday on May 15, 2005. With ten decades of decadence and a world-famous image under its belt, Sin City must be doing something right. I can only hope I look that good when I turn 100!

A Man's Man
Las Vegas History

L et's consider a man's man history of Las Vegas, which is sure to
stir the imagination of every red-blooded male who's ever visited Sin City. It all started way back in 1829, when Antonio
Armijo, a Mexican trader, led a sixty-person-strong man's man crew
along the old Spanish Trail to Los Angeles, California. During their
travels, they veered off the regular route. Armijo and his men decided to set up camp about 100 miles northeast of Las Vegas. A small
scouting group rode west to look for water. Something urged Rafael
Rivera (a savvy Mexican scout) to leave his fellow men and travel into
unknown desert territory. What was the result? Rivera discovered
Las Vegas Springs. He became the very first non-Indian to set foot in
the now-world-famous Las Vegas Valley. Now, that's a man's man!

The story of the modern, flashy Las Vegas really started back in
the mid 1940s when mobster Benjamin "Bugsy" Siegel developed his
dream of building a gambling resort in the desert. The $6 million
Flamingo Hotel (known today as the Flamingo Hilton) was con-

structed as the centerpiece, backed by East Coast mob money. Siegel had some serious dreams of instant wealth, but unfortunately the project didn't turn a profit as quickly as its backers anticipated, and Siegel was "terminated" on June 23, 1947.

But, the man's man entrepreneurial momentum had started in Las Vegas and continued to move ahead full force. Gus Greenbaum took over control of the wavering Flamingo Hotel, and it reopened to rave reviews and achieved big success for years to come. By the 1950s, Las Vegas resembled a virtual boomtown with hotels like the lavish Desert Inn (costing close to $5 million) setting the pace.

There's no doubt that the "Rat Pack" era brought about a more swinging and glamorous image for Las Vegas. Frank Sinatra, of course, was never a stranger to the desert destination. He first became acquainted with the Nevada town when he appeared in an almost forgotten Paramount movie called *Las Vegas Nights* in his real-life role as the singing star of the top big band of the day, the Tommy Dorsey Orchestra.

In September of 1951, Sinatra started his first genuine Las Vegas live gig, debuting at the Desert Inn during a time when there were only a half-dozen hotels on the strip. Professional journalists have said that outside of gambling, there's been no single entity as beneficial to Las Vegas as Frank Sinatra. Sinatra's overwhelming success influenced the most famous names in the music business to perform in Las Vegas—Nat "King" Cole, Peggy Lee, Dean Martin, Sammy Davis, Jr., Louis Prima, and Keely Smith all became top draws in nightclubs there.

Yes, Sinatra set the standard when he played at the Desert Inn, and later at the Sands (his best-remembered fourteen-year onstage tour of duty), both relatively early in the game. A treasured man's man "collectible" of that era is the 1966 Reprise Records album *Sinatra at the Sands*, produced live on-location by Sonny Burke and arranged and conducted by man's man Quincy Jones. That album highlights one of the final major appearances of "Ol' Blue Eyes" at the legendary Sands. Much later in his Las Vegas career, Sinatra injected his special brand of magic to the MGM Grand, the Golden Nugget, and Bally's. In all, Sinatra was a "sold-out" Las Vegas headliner for over forty years, and attracted high-rollers and free-spending tourists from all over the world with his unique blend of talent and charisma.

However, from all accounts, it was Frank Sinatra combined with the infamous Rat Pack—Sinatra, Dean Martin, Sammy Davis Jr., Peter Lawford and Joey Bishop—on stage at the Sands that made the gambling mecca a man's man kind of town for decades to follow.

Let's turn the pages back to early 1960s Las Vegas for a moment. By day, Academy Award–winning director Lewis Milestone was overseeing the filming of a major motion picture production, *Oceans 11*, starring Sinatra, Martin, Davis, Lawford, and Bishop. By night, the same group of stars electrified the stage at the Sands with the coolest act in show business history. Sinatra and his buddies became the kings of Las Vegas with nightly shows that brought in the likes of everyone from soon-to-be-president John F. Kennedy to movie queens like Marilyn Monroe to television titans like Milton Berle; anyone who was anyone flocked to Sin City to fully enjoy the phenomena called the Rat Pack!

In 1966, a new "sheriff" landed in Las Vegas—eccentric man's man billionaire Howard Hughes. Hughes truly wrote the

MEMORABLE MAN'S MAN MOMENTS IN LAS VEGAS HISTORY

1931—Gambling is legalized in Nevada.

1946—Mobster "Bugsy" Siegel opens the Flamingo Hotel on the Strip.

1951—Frank Sinatra makes his first Vegas appearance at the Desert Inn.

1957—Minsky's Follies premieres as the first topless show in Las Vegas history.

1960—The Rat Pack performs their first show at the Sands.

1969—Elvis Presley marries Priscilla at the Aladdin Hotel.

1995—Martin Scorsese's epic Las Vegas motion picture *Casino* hits theaters nationwide.

2005—Las Vegas turns 100 years old.

book on putting one's money where one's mouth is. Certainly we have all heard of the stories about Howard Hughes reinventing Las Vegas from his posh suite high atop the Desert Inn. I guess Hughes really liked Vegas, because he went on a multimillion-dollar spending spree that encompassed purchasing various key hotels like the Sands, Desert Inn, New Frontier, Silver Slipper, and Landmark, as well as a television station and land including the North Las Vegas Airport. Wow! When this man's man went on a shopping spree, he really went on a shopping spree! And Hughes arrived in Las Vegas in the back of an ambulance, with no fanfare whatsoever. Talk about low-key.

Man's man entertainer Elvis Presley also had a major effect on Vegas, helping to establish it as the "The Entertainment Capital of the World" that it's considered today. Elvis definitely brought excitement back to the desert. It first started when Elvis married Priscilla in a big event hosted by Milton Prell at his Aladdin Hotel (imploded in 1998). The private ceremony was performed May 1, 1967, by Nevada Supreme Court Justice David Zenoff. Then, Elvis was booked for the opening night at Kirk Kerkorian's International Hotel on July 26, 1969, a major VIP event. Elvis took to the stage and, from all accounts, delivered the most impressive "Blue Suede Shoes" rendition ever heard. Elvis went on to appear there for a four-week gig twice a year (fifty-seven-show engagement) at a salary of $125,000 per week.

Although the movie *Viva Las Vegas* is best known for featuring "the King," my buddies and I were more closely watching his co-star in that flick, a major "hottie" of the era, Ann-Margret. Which leads me to the fact that beautiful women and Las Vegas seem to have always gone hand-in-hand, from the dynamite showgirls to the lovely female visitors who frequent the city. The ultimate man's man, "Chairman of the Board" Frank Sinatra, even married one of the most gorgeous former showgirls who ever graced a Vegas stage, the lovely Barbara. I guess that says it all!

A man's man history would not be complete without mentioning some more of the city's gutsy entrepreneurs who are still taking big gambles and making major moves in Sin City. Acknowledged as the

genuine "father of the Las Vegas mega-resort," Kirk Kerkorian was
the son of Armenian parents who spoke English as his second language growing up. Though he dropped out of junior high school, he
parlayed two and a half years of top-dollar earnings piloting newly
manufactured Royal Air Force planes during World War II into a
Las Vegas hotel, an international airline, and Hollywood movie studio investments. That eventually made him the forty-first richest
man in the USA, worth about $5.7 billion. He is a *true* American suc-
cess story. He contributed his vision and business sense toward creat-
ing the MGM Grand Hotel, and opened that legendary Las Vegas
landmark with Barbra Streisand starring in the main showroom of
the then "largest hotel in the world." As one of the key men's men
who shaped modern Las Vegas, Kerkorian, at close to ninety years
old, is still a "player" and is as bullish about Vegas' future prospects
today as he was back in 1945.

The impact of man's man Steve Wynn on Las Vegas is truly monumental. Wynn first visited Vegas as a wide-eyed ten-year-old with
his father back in 1952. It was man's man Vegas banker-turned-
mentor, E. Parry Thomas, who believed in Wynn and loaned him the
money to launch his casino empire. Old-time Golden Nugget owner
"Bucky" Blaine sold out to Wynn, who skillfully used his University
of Pennsylvania and Wharton Business School backgrounds to increase pre-tax profits there threefold, from $1.1 million to $4.2 million. Wynn built another successful Golden Nugget in Atlantic City
(capitalizing on Frank Sinatra's image, performance power, and TV
commercials along with jets, helicopters and limos to bring in high-
rollers). Then came the Wynn-conceived Bellagio Hotel and Resort.
Its priceless collection of museum-quality art was the cornerstone of
another major success story. The Bellagio set the stage for Steve
Wynn's newest venture: the Wynn Las Vegas, the record-setting $2.7
billion hotel-resort with a 150-foot man-made mountain out in front,
which opened in 2005.

Today, even decades after Sinatra's Rat Pack and Elvis wowed audiences in the "desert of dreams," the man's man aura is still alive in

Vegas. Even though the entertainers' names have changed and many old hotels have been replaced, some things have stayed the same. Take the world-class prizefights, for example. Vegas has been the site of some of the most legendary boxing events ever. Fighters like Jack Dempsey and Jack Johnson (the first black heavyweight champion, in 1910) took on opponents there as early as the 1900s. But, it was the advent of closed-circuit television that revolutionized the sport of boxing, and Las Vegas was the center of the action, continuing to host the most exciting boxing matches in the world. The great boxers who stepped into the ring in Vegas include Evander Holyfield, George Foreman, Smokin' Joe Frazier, Michael Spinks, Sugar Ray Leonard, and my top boxing idol of all time, Muhammad Ali. These boxers are truly reflective of the overall man's man history of Las Vegas—people fighting to get a piece of the American dream.

Top Ten Man's Man Hotels

The Bellagio

First opened: 1998

Major attraction: The Bellagio's world-famous fountains, which are choreographed to opera and classical music. It's a great place for a romantic kiss after dinner.

Ambiance: Tuscan villa in the desert.

Location: 3600 Las Vegas Blvd. South (right on the Strip, across from the Paris and next to Caesar's Palace).

Contact Info: 888-987-3456, www.bellagio.com

Resting Your Head: Surround yourself in a AAA Five Diamond Award–winning enhanced room with European style. Then, peer out your window at the man's man view of the exhilarating Las Vegas Strip that will make you feel like the king of Sin City. The view of Paris across the street, the view of the Caesar's Pool (binoculars not included), and the constant roar of the breathtaking outdoor fountains make this hotel unforgettable. Did I forget to tell you about the decadently stocked minibars for pre-party action and electronic drapes for post-party action? That's Man's Man 101. With guest rooms and suites ranging from 853 square feet to 2,050 square feet, there's more than enough space to kick back and chill. Also, many rooms include a steam shower, which is prime to loosen up those sore muscles after a day of golf. Let me tell ya, there's nothing like resting your head in a hotel that cost $1.6 billion to build!

Recover: Go to the Bellagio's elaborate spa, which is located beyond the breathtaking indoor garden. Here, indulge yourself with the "Bellagio's Royal Shave," definitely something the true man's man Vegas pacesetter, Frank Sinatra, would have done in a heartbeat. Service begins with a steamed hot towel and ends with natural sea sponges soaked in lemon and essential oils. They offer a thirty-minute service ($35) and a forty-five-minute service ($50). They also offer aromatherapy skin treatment, which seems kind of feminine, but when your lady is all over your skin that night telling you how soft it feels, you'll be back for more!

Dining/Entertainment: Have the Bellagio concierge book you tickets to Cirque Du Soleil's *O*. This is something you may want to do in advance, because the show is extremely popular. The tickets are a tad pricey, but a man's man pays no mind when he's in Vegas. This hotel has some of the best restaurants in town. Make sure you have your sport coat pressed and your black AmEx card shiny when you dine at Picasso. The restaurant is known not only for its French-Mediterranean cuisine, but also for its authentic and original artwork. Need to make up with your significant other because you spent all day in the casino and only five minutes with her in the pool? Head over to Jasmine—the restaurant's sparkling chandeliers and beautiful flowers are built for romance. Case closed—you're forgiven. If traveling with the boys, or if your woman likes to hit the dance floor and "shake what her mama gave her," head over to club Light where you can get a private table and a man's man view of the action.

Gaming: This might be the most action-packed casino floor in all of Las Vegas. Whether you are interested in betting your bank account or just playing for fun, Bellagio offers an array of table games. The choices are: blackjack, roulette, craps, Caribbean Stud, Let it Ride Stud Poker, pai gow tiles, pai gow poker, Big Six, Three-Card Poker, baccarat, and Texas Hold 'Em.

Shopping: The Via Bellagio is the crème de la crème of shopping venues. Giorgio Armani, Chanel, Dior, and Gucci are all there. Need I say more? It's high style all the way, fellas.

The Wynn

First Opened: 2005

Main Attraction: The on-site eighteen-hole championship golf course (with a thirty-seven-foot waterfall on the eighteenth hole) designed by Tom Fazio and Steve Wynn, coupled with the man-made mountain that towers in front of the hotel.

Ambiance: Pure sophistication and luxury.

Location: 3131 Las Vegas Blvd. South (adjacent to the Treasure Island Hotel and across from the Fashion Show Mall).

Contact Info: 888-320-9966, www.wynnlasvegas.com

Resting Your Head: This hotel might have the best accommodations in all of Las Vegas. If you are into golfing, I suggest staying in the Fairway Villas in either a one-bedroom (starting at $1,200) or a two-bedroom (starting at $1,700). Both rooms overlook the golf course. However, for the non-golfing traveler, I personally recommend staying in the Salon Suite. The Salon Suite has an incredible view of the Las Vegas Strip, and guests have the option to choose the color scheme of the room they are staying in. The color schemes are as follows: Chocolate Cherry (consists of deep-red velvet couch and coordinating drapes) and Carnelian Crème (rustic wall color with crème-accented furniture). Your lady's gonna love it!

Recover: With five pools (one dedicated to the suites only), you'll be a man's man "of the world" as you take a dip in pure luxury. The spa in the beauty shop offers treatment rooms, beauty products, and an amazing staff for your full enjoyment. Want good luck for your night of gambling? This hotel actually performs spa "rituals." The "Good Luck Ritual" treatment is based on the five areas of feng shui—happiness, harmony, wealth, health, and prosperity. It's a fifty-minute custom massage. Hey, for $250 a pop, you better be lucky at the tables after that rubdown! Seriously, it's worth every penny, fellas. Wynn Las Vegas also offers forty-five treatment rooms, showers, sauna, steam room, and whirlpool. You want some recovery room service? If a man's man is tired, he can have the spa come to him. "In-room" massages run for either sixty minutes ($165) or ninety minutes ($265).

Dining/Entertainment: At the theater there's the French show *Le Reve*, which translated into English means "The Dream." There's also the award-winning musical *Avenue Q*. This hotel has its very own golf course with an amazing landscape, so you can enjoy an eighteen-hole game with the boys right on the premises! If you forget your golf gear, go to the pro shop, which sells everything from golf accessories and apparel to premium cigars and humidors. Nice! After a fulfilling day beating all your buddies at golf, you'll surely have worked up an appetite. At the Wynn Las Vegas, the focus is not only on the restaurants but on the star chefs who are preparing the meals. Want fine Italian cuisine? Look no further than Bartolotta Ristorante Di Mare. Chef Paul Bartolotta will personally prepare you one of his signature dishes. They don't fool around here. In fact, they fly ingredients in daily, such as seafood directly from Europe. Have a sweet tooth? Indulge at Chocolat, executive pastry chef Frederic Robert's pastry heaven. The secret ingredient of all the Wynn hotel restaurants is that these well-known chefs are actually on the premises and in the kitchen, preparing and cooking these one-of-a-kind meals. Now, after dinner, a man's man will definitely go to Wynn's hot nightclub Lure. Crack open a bottle of bubbly and really let loose. No hats, jeans, or athletic wear allowed, so you know the clientele is going to be exclusively man's man caliber.

Gaming: The Wynn offers many games of chance for a man's man. Try betting on a horse or your favorite sports team in the sports book area within the ultimate lounge setting. They also have 1,900 slot games to choose from. The poker room has such popular games as Texas Hold 'Em, Seven-Card Stud, Hi-Low and more; players are offered pot-limit and no-limit games. From blackjack to Big 6 to craps to roulette, a man's man will be able to keep himself busy at the Wynn Casino for sure!

Shopping: This hotel has the ultimate as far as upscale shopping goes. It offers everything from Louis Vuitton, Dior, Chanel, Cartier, to Brioni and probably anything else your heart or your lady's heart desires. Let's face it, a man's man definitely has a need for speed. So, if you get *very* lucky at the tables, waltz on over to the Ferrari/Maserati showroom and check out the best rides in the world. It's only man's man territory at the Wynn.

The Venetian

First Opened: 1999

Major Attraction: Every room is a suite.

Ambiance: Old-world Venice.

Location: 3355 Las Vegas Blvd. South (across from the Mirage and next to Harrah's).

Contact Info: 877-427-7243, www.venetian.com

Resting Your Head: The Venetian's man's man draw is that every room is a suite. Which means every man is treated like a king! The décor of each room is very sexy, with red velvet drapes everywhere. The new wing, Venezia at the Venetian, offers even more amenities and more spacious rooms than the first phase of the hotel. Of these, fourteen of the suites on the pool level include elaborate private trellises, offering privacy for the most discerning guests (a.k.a hook-up heaven!).

Recover: At the Canyon Ranch Spa Club (named one of the top seven spas in the United States) you can test your testosterone level with a rock climb, and afterward unwind with a rubdown and steam in the sauna to get rejuvenated for the long night ahead. At the Venetian and its concierge-level Venezia Hotel, you have the choice of two pools. The first pool is located off the fourth floor of the Venetian, and is surrounded by private cabanas, two hot tubs, and outdoor showers. If you want some real "privacy," reserve an outdoor private cabana which will run you anywhere from $150 to $300 per day. At the Venezia Tower, enjoy the Pool Garden Courtyard, which is located on the ground floor and is flanked by some ritzy suites.

Dining/Entertainment: The indoor gondola ride at the Grand Canal will have you and your lady fooled (if just for a moment) that you're really in Venice. There is so much to choose from as far as great dining is concerned. For a gourmet man's man hamburger, hit the Solaro Café (from Wolfgang Puck's Postrio). If you truly like to eat, look no further than the hotel's Delmonico Steakhouse, Postrio, and Valentino's (with a man's man wine list offering over 24,000 bottles to choose from). Stroll into Zeffirino and savor the best brunch in Las Vegas, hands down.

Gaming: After a juicy filet mignon at Delmonico (winner of the James Beard Award), stroll over to the casino for an evening with lady luck. The Venetian offers lavish surroundings while you play some of their top table games like craps, baccarat, pai gow, poker, roulette, three-card Poker, Casino War, Caribbean Stud, and more! The beautiful cocktail waitresses keep the drinks coming. Hopefully, the money will be coming, too.

Shopping: A 500,000-square-foot luxury shopping experience awaits you. If you were lucky at the tables, head over to famed jewelers Chopar, Concord, and Rado for some new cuff links for yourself, and something hot for your special someone.

Mandalay Bay Resort & Casino

First opened: 1999

Main Attraction: Eleven-acre tropical lagoon with realistic waves.

Ambiance: Tropical oasis.

Location: 3950 Las Vegas Blvd. South (on the south side of the Luxor Hotel)

Contact info: 877-632-7800, www.mandalaybay.com

Resting Your Head: The Mandalay Bay (which cost $1.5 billion to build) still reserves its most exclusive suites for high-rollers. However, you can stay at its luxury adjacent digs, called THEhotel. This "all-suite" tower has a private entrance with completely separate check-in, lounge spots, and eatery. The suites (750 square feet apiece) priced from $179 to $399, are decorated with man's man dark rich furniture, floor-to-ceiling windows, and twenty-seven-inch flat screen TVs for your viewing pleasure.

Recover: Ready for your rubdown, men? Cruise over to the 30,000-square-foot world-class Spa Mandalay—a complete relaxation mecca offering rejuvenation of the mind, body, and spirit. Hey, are you dreaming of a two-on-one? Look no further than the Massage in Tandem. This spa service offers two massage therapists for fifty minutes, for $205. A great treat for the lady in your life is an appointment for a stylish haircut at the Robert Cromeans Salon, followed by a unique Floral Fantasy pedicure at the Salon Mandalay. If you're in the doghouse for some reason, this will get you out for sure! No hotel pool in Vegas compares to the tropical sand beach (with simulated ocean waves) at the Mandalay Bay. With three pools (open from 9 A.M. to 5 P.M.), there's enough water to go around.

Dining/Entertainment: A man's man always has a yen for a quality burger. So, bring your appetite to the Burger Bar (located in Mandalay Place) and enjoy that juicy meat with a side of crisp potatoes. If you are in Vegas on business, you should schedule your dinner meeting at the swanky 3950 Restaurant. Want to really impress those clients with a hard-core appetizer that starts things right and really sets the pace? A man's man orders the Seafood on Ice ($85) for openers, which contains oysters, clams, chilled Maine lobster, jumbo shrimp, and savory sauce. Make a reservation because this place is *very* popular. Missing that New York City flavor? Book a table at Aureole, modeled after Charlie Palmer's famous NYC spot, which features a four-story wine tower. The professional boxing matches are always a big draw at Mandalay Bay. Also, make sure not to miss the live acts at the House of Blues. Or, bring the love of your life to a smash-hit show like *Mama Mia* and make it a Vegas night to remember. One of Vegas's best nightspots is in Mandalay Bay. It has great music, many larger-than-life waterfalls and tropical drinks to get your date feeling good. The next day you should go to the million-and-a-half-gallon Shark Reef aquarium, where you can see some of the most dangerous sharks in the world. Man's man or not, thank God they are behind thick, thick glass!

Gaming: Test your luck in a tropical setting of palm trees and flowing water. Blackjack minimum bet is $5 and maximum bet is $10,000 (if you're rolling hard). When you are playing at one of the tables, order your favorite man's man drink (on the house, and only name-brand alcohol served) from one of the friendly Mandalay Bay waitresses. They also have a race and sports book where you can not only bet on your favorite team, but also root them on on one of the seventeen large screens.

Shopping: The Bali Trading Company has some great home décor items like cool accent tables, frames, and many jewelry boxes to choose from for your lady. For some fine art, peruse the world-renowned Jack Gallery. Need some poolside attire because the airline lost your luggage? Surf Shack has got it all—swimsuits, hats, shades, flip-flops, and more. Also, go to the Wave for the top golf shirt brand names all in one place. Remember that a man's man always surprises his lady with fresh flowers while on vacation. So, smell the roses at Mandalay Bay Floral and put your money where your mouth is. She'll love you for it, guaranteed!

The Palms Hotel

First Opened: 2002

Main Attraction: Constant party atmosphere prevails at the hotel's top clubs, Rain and Ghostbar.

Ambiance: Futuristic cool.

Location: 4321 West Domingo (off the Strip, across from the Rio Hotel)

Contact Info: 866-942-7770, www.palms.com

Resting Your Head: Honestly, there will be probably very little resting at this party hotel. If you feel like being a celebrity during your stay in Sin City, look no further than the "Real World" Suite. At an impressive 2,900 square feet and $7,500 per night, you will be partying harder than a rock star. There are also rooms called the Play Pens. What does that mean? Use your man's man imagination and figure it out for yourself! These suites (decorated in a '60s vibe) offer bachelor and bachelorette accommodations complete with stripper poles, a dance floor and a sound system that will blow your mind. Also, the NBA Suites cater to those men's men who have big hands and are very tall, boasting ten-foot ceilings and extra-large beds. Maybe you'll get some rest in Vegas after all.

Recover: The 18,000-square-foot spa (open 6 A.M. to 8 P.M. daily) features whirlpools, steam, sauna, cold plunges, and other man's man offerings. The state-of-the-art fitness center overlooks the swimming pool. Nothing like a good view while running like a maniac on the treadmill! The couples' massage room is a great place to unwind and loosen up with the lady in your life. I gotta recommend the

Southwest Stone Therapy. It relieves stress, tense muscles, and sore joints. Remember, a man's man must keep an open mind to new experiences. Want to cool off? Aptly called the "Skin Pool Lounge," this 75,000-square-foot man's man oasis offers private cabanas, outdoor blackjack, poolside massages, and a bevy of beauties you'll wish you could rub some SPF 30 on.

Dining/Entertainment: If you would like to impress a date or just get a first-class meal with some of your buddies, you gotta dine at Alizé. It's gourmet French dining at its best with an intense panoramic view of *all* of Vegas. There's also N9NE Steakhouse, which is where the beef's at! Prime aged steak, fresh seafood, and an exclusive champagne and caviar bar are among its highlights. The modern décor makes you feel like you are "in the know." It received 2005's coveted The Best of Las Vegas Award in the highly respected *Las Vegas Review Journal* poll. Another restaurant at the Palms with a little "Asian persuasion" is Little Buddha (restaurant, sushi bar, and lounge). The sizes of the portions are only outdone by the Buddha statue you pass on your way in! Now, after you eat at one of these top eateries you can work off the meal at one of two hot nightclubs right at the Palms. The first, Rain, is a 28,000-square-foot playground, which has hosted such top acts as Jay-Z, Carlos Santana, Seal, and too many more famous names to mention. Skyboxes and cabanas provide some privacy for you and that special someone from the crowds on the dance floor. The second, Ghostbar, gives you a view of the whole Strip from fifty-five floors above. Also, from the "ghostdeck" there's another amazing outdoor view via a see-through acrylic floor looking right down at the Skin Pool Lounge. This is man's man clubbing at its very best.

Gaming: With over 2,000 slots and video poker machines, a keno lounge, and all the table games a man's man could desire housed in a 95,000-square-foot casino, you'll probably end up hanging out in this section of the hotel during much of your stay.

Shopping: The Palms Shop has logo clothing, dress clothes for club wear by designers like Kenneth Cole, and also women's lingerie and kinky merchandise if you're in the mood. Also, check out the Palms' gift shop called Stuff.

Caesar's Palace

First Opened: 1966

Major Attraction: Celine Dion extravaganza housed in the $95 million Colosseum (built just for her show).

Ambiance: Neo-Roman Empire.

Location: 3570 Las Vegas Boulevard South (next to the Mirage in the heart of the Strip).

Contact Info: 877-427-7243, www.caesarspalace.com

Resting your Head: Some rooms include large whirlpool tubs (in case you have twins as company), European-style marble bathrooms, elegant armoires, dressing rooms, sitting and desk areas, guest safes (to keep your money stash), and small refrigerators (to keep your beer stash). If you forgot to press your best shirt, no worries, because all rooms come equipped with ironing boards and irons. Don't be shy, take advantage of round-the-clock room service.

Recover: A man's man can really kick back at Caesar's. Their top-notch spa and fitness center offers a full array of relaxation services. They have massages, body treatments, wraps, salt glows, baths, a co-ed relaxation room (a man's man loves anything coed), and more.

Looking to recharge with a healthy fruit drink (and I don't mean Absolut Mandarin)? Their juice bar has got everything, including outdoor terrace seating, overlooking the Garden of the Gods Pool Oasis. The pool is an ode to the Greek gods. Unfortunately, the naked statues are predominantly male, but the scantily-clad women poolside more than make up for it. Hotel facilities include men's and women's whirlpools, steam rooms, saunas, tanning booths, gym and a rock-climbing wall (for those who are too chicken to attempt the Grand Canyon).

Dining/Entertainment: I suggest trying restaurants in the Forum Mall in Caesar's Palace. If you're on a date with a "ten," I recommend Spago (a true Beverly Hills classic transplanted to Vegas), Palm Restaurant, or Il Mulino New York. If you're dating a "six," I recommend the Cheescake Factory and if she's a "four," do a plate share. *Mangia!*

Gaming: Are you into slot machines? Well, Caesar's Palace offers a wide variety of slot machines in denominations raging from 5 cents (monopolized by old little ladies from Pasadena) to $500 (played by men's men from Beverly Hills). In fact, Caesar's Palace has been the site of more million-dollar-plus slot machine jackpots than any casino in the world! Other games include blackjack, dice, roulette, baccarat, Spanish 21, mini-baccarat, pai gow and pai gow poker. Also, check out the Caesar's Palace Race and Sports Book to let it ride on your favorite thoroughbred or sports team.

Shopping: With more than 160 boutiques and stores, your lady and your credit card are sure to have a strenuous workout. If flying solo, the Versace store will outfit you in something that'll be sure to attract all the women.

The Hard Rock Hotel

First Opened: 1995

Major Attraction: Performances by today's most famous musical artists, memorabilia from yesterday's biggest musical artists, and the sexiest pool atmosphere in all of Las Vegas.

Ambiance: Rock 'n' roll meets art deco.

Location: 4455 Paradise Road (off the Strip. Atrium Suites Hotel is next door, and the topless Club Paradise is across the street.)

Contact Info: 800-HRD-ROCK, www.hardrockhotel.com

Resting Your Head: There are many different stylish and sleek rooms to choose from. But, the man's man options are clear: The Celebrity Suite (1,300 square feet, starting at $550 per night) screams "bachelor pad" with its plush suede sofas; the Penthouse Suite (3,500 square feet, costing $5,000 per night) has three huge bedrooms, view of the Strip from your mosaic hot tub, and an actual single-lane bowling alley. Wow! The Boom Boom Room (1,300 square feet, starting at $1,000 per night) has a pool table, state-of-the-art sound system, overstuffed leather couches, bar, and stripper pole built in for all your bachelor party desires. (Sorry, strippers not included.)

Recover: After a night of man's man debauchery, drag your ass over to the Rock Spa for some R&R. This spa offers an array of massages, wraps, and facials. The spa is designed to protect your body from stress inducers—just what you need before you head out for another night of craziness with your fellow men's men! Oh, by the way, get pumped up at the health club. Inside, there are flat-screen TVs everywhere, but you won't be watching them with all the incredible eye candy on the treadmills. Last, but *certainly not least*, the Hard Rock Hotel Beach Club it a must-see. It's got more silicone than Silicon Valley. The palm-shaded sandy-beached pools are known to house the most beautiful bodies from all corners of the world. Swim up to the pool bar and sip on a cocktail while you're working on that tan, boys. Also, if you like to gamble while in the water, backstroke over to Hard Rock's Poolside Palapa and play some blackjack. If you feel like reminiscing about your trip afterwards, be sure to check out the website's cams, which take live pictures of the pool area.

Dining/Entertainment: Are you in the mood for sushi in a trendy atmosphere? Nobu is the answer, serving some of the best sushi in Las Vegas (flown in fresh daily from the Tokyo fish market). Take in some live piano while enjoying a juicy steak over at AJ's Streakhouse, which is also known for its unbeatable martinis. The place oozes "cool." With its weekday happy hour and margarita specials (remember, a man's man only drinks them on the rocks), the hotel's Pink Taco offers some of the best authentic Mexican food Sin City has to offer. Now, picture this . . . It's 11 P.M. and you just won big at the craps table. Get the gang and head over to the nightclub Body English to celebrate. With a cover charge of $30 for gentleman and $20 for ladies, don't "bring sand to the beach." Fly solo, guys, because there are many fine ladies already working it on the dance floor.

Gaming: In a truly stylish atmosphere you can bet at top table games like roulette, pai gow poker, blackjack, craps, and others while smoking your stogie. Join the Backstage Pass Player's Club and earn points by playing the tables and slots where winnings can be used for hotel rooms, merchandise, "comp" dinners, and other fun.

Shopping: Sure it's a guilty pleasure, but everyone who visits a Hard Rock establishment succumbs to purchasing some form of Hard Rock product. Get a stylish tank top for your lady—a little thought goes a long way. Also, just in case you're in a big spending mood, I want to tell about two places. First, head over to Rocks the Jewelers for some major bling-bling. Then, I suggest you go to Love Jones Lingerie, because that store has everything to make your woman feel sexy and beautiful. Let's face it guys, when she's happy, you're happy.

The MGM Grand

First Opened: 1993

Main Attraction: The largest casino in the world and the biggest hotel in the United States.

Ambiance: Hollywood meets Vegas.

Location: 3977 Las Vegas Blvd. South (right across from the New York, New York and the Tropicana).

Contact Info: 877-880-0880, www.mgmgrand.com

Resting Your Head: Want to go hard-core man's man? I'm talking top-of-the-line accommodations. At the MGM Grand, there is a private building called "The Mansion." It actually looks like a real mansion, complete with clear white lights highlighting all of its architecture. A one-bedroom villa (2,400 square feet) starts at $5,000 per night. A two-bedroom villa (3,600 square feet) is $6,000 a night. "Private" everything rules here—spa, casino, pool, butler, dining, etc. Also, there's a Rolls Royce on call at all times for when you're ready to go out on the town. A man's man knows all about the benefits of having the Centurian AmEx (black AmEx). Use your Centurian card when you book your room and get credits for free dinners, spa treatments, and free show tickets. The décor here is like nothing you've ever seen. If your wallet isn't that thick, stay in a Terrace Suite, which is 1,300 square feet, costing $1,000 per night. And don't worry—just because it costs less than the Mansion doesn't mean the perks are any less spectacular. In your Terrace Suite, sit in your Jacuzzi on your own private patio with a view of the Strip. Two-story vaulted ceilings and a dining room are some of the other available amenities. I also recommend the Sky Lofts. The Sky Lofts are the original penthouse rooms of the hotel, but have been completely refurbished and redesigned. I recommend a one-bedroom loft (1,400 square feet) starting at $1,800 a night. The views are insane! Since Vegas is a twenty-four-hour town, this hotel supplies an espresso machine in each sky loft room.

Recover: Feel like the King and Queen of Vegas when you're visiting the Grand Spa. You'll be surrounded by rare sculptures, waterfalls, and soft music that can even put the most hard-core party guy to sleep. Want to treat your woman to something different? Buy her the "Buff and Bronze" package and she'll be sporting a sweet golden tan (and you'll be golden as you get an extra hour at the casino to win big). Want another hour at the Casino alone? Send her over to the legendary celebrity hair stylist Cristophe of the Cristophe Salon. This guy styles the hair of many top celebs, and now your lucky lady can get the same star treatment ($400 a cut and style, but book a month in advance). Sure, it'll cost you, but a man's man sometimes has to give a little to get a little free time at the casino. Don't forget to cool off in one of the MGM Grand's five pools and unwind in one of their many whirlpools in a man's man tropical environment.

Dining/Entertainment: If you want to have a complete man's man evening at the MGM Grand, then listen up: first, book a couple of seats in advance to the special *KÀ* show of the world-famous Cirque du Soleil. Take in this show with a hot date and enjoy a one-of-a-kind acrobatic and martial arts performance. Next, "kick it up a notch" with chef Emeril at Emeril's restaurant and enjoy some good ol' Cajun cuisine. It's simply the tops. Think the night's over? I don't think so. We've got Tabu on the roster. It's an ultra-hip lounge with enough champagne to quench your thirst and then some. Now, a man's man always knows how to be discreet. If you're with a date, do not gawk at the stunning model/hostesses at this trendy hangout. Now that you and your date are all warm and fuzzy from the champagne, you can relive the days of the hot, hot Studio 54 at MGM's club appropriately called Studio 54. Awesome music and some interesting characters running around this 22,000-square-foot pleasure dome make it one colorful nightspot.

Gaming: First of all, this is the largest casino in the world. That's got man's man written all over it! If you're into slots, the denominations go from 5 cents to $500. Want a chance to win $1,000,000? Take a pull on the Lion's Share slot machine. Table games include blackjack, roulette, baccarat, pai gow tiles, pai gow poker, craps, Spanish 21, Casino War, big six, Three-Card Poker, Caribbean Stud, and Let It Ride Stud Poker. Also, the twenty-three-table (nonsmoking) Poker Room is open twenty-four hours a day.

Shopping: Since you're already at the MGM Grand, you have to go to its very stylish store Bernini. It's a must! With designer names like Versace, Armani, Brioni, and Canali (just to name a few), it's true man's man territory. Shoes? Ferragamo is the answer. You are stylin' now with only the primo Italian footwear and clothing at your fingertips.

The Paris

First Opened: 1999

Ambiance: Paris in the desert.

Main Attraction: Las Vegas's version of the Eiffel Tower and the Arc de Triomphe.

Location: 3655 Las Vegas Blvd. (in between the Alladin and Bally's, across from the Bellagio).

Contact Info: 888-Bon-Jour, www.parislasvegas.com

Resting Your Head: With its traditional French décor, the Nice Suite (1,160 square feet) is very relaxing and low-key. The room starts at $1,139 a night and comes complete with bar, formal dining area, and Jacuzzi tub. Man's man advice: Request a room facing the Eiffel Tower so you can also enjoy the impressive fountains at the neighboring Bellagio and an awesome view of the Strip. With the hotel housing 2,916 rooms, there will be many loving couples strolling the terrain both indoor and out, a perfect setting for *l'amour*, as the French say.

Recover: Is your arm a little sore from pulling the slots till sunup? No problem. The Paris Spa by Mandara has the answer. When you walk into this 26,000-square-foot Bali-influenced haven, see the check-in person and get booked for one of the spa's twenty-four amazing treatment rooms. The massages, which use authentic Balinese-based techniques, are sure to have you on the mend in no time. Personal training services are also available at the state-of-the-art Mandara Fitness Center. You can work out with the trainer and get your body buff and strong. (Every man's man knows that women like men who take care of themselves.) While you sunbathe beside the huge replica of the Eiffel Tower, you'll probably think you're in Paris, even if just for a brief moment. The two-acre rooftop pool is appropriately set in a French garden. Want to impress that woman you met last night at the craps table? Get the "his and hers" poolside massage. That's sure to make any women melt in your hands. A man's man knows when he has to show his generous side, and this is right on the money.

Dining/Entertainment: Looking for an awesome view and five-star food? Look no further than this great "date" restaurant. The

Eiffel Tower restaurant is located inside the hotel's landmark replica. This restaurant is run by Chef J. Joho, who prepares acclaimed French cuisine. This eatery has one of the most romantic views of Las Vegas—a great spot if you are looking to take a leap of faith and propose to your soul mate. I have to say I found this next restaurant, Ortanique, quite interesting. The food is Caribbean cuisine prepared in the French style, combining fresh, natural ingredients with exotic, tropical flavors to create dishes that are fantastic. After-dinner drinks is a Vegas pasttime; so is smoking a great cigar. Napoleon's has both and a melodic live jazz band to boot. Napoleon's is Las Vegas's pre-miere champagne bar. In addition to a full-service bar and more than one hundred carefully selected varieties of champagne ready to be enjoyed, it features a fully-stocked cigar humidor. Just another rea-son why this is a place you must visit! Ready to dance the night away? There is a wild vibe over at the Parisian hot spot, "Risqué" at "Paris Las Vegas." At this super chic lounge/club, enjoy a fine collection of wines, champagnes, and cocktails, all from a balcony view of the Las Vegas Strip! Hey, the French aren't the only nightlife seekers! Watch out, buddy, here I come! Finish the night off with a romantic walk around Paris with your lady, taking in the gorgeous re-creations of the Arc de Triomphe, the Eiffel Tower, the Louvre, the Paris Opera House and the Hôtel de Ville. Don't know what these sites are? Well, I guess you didn't do too well in your history class. My suggestion: Hop a plane to Vegas and take the crash course at the Paris Hotel.

Gaming: The casino has over ninety tables with various man's man games like blackjack, craps, baccarat, mini-baccarat, roulette, and others. The Paris also offers two top man's man poker games—Texas Hold 'Em and seven-card stud. Or go over to the sports book, grab a drink at the bar and throw some cash on your favorite team. You can bet anything you like, from a basic moneyline wager to an elaborate ten-team parlay. With multiple big-screen televisions as well as indi-vidual television monitors, you won't miss any of the action at the Paris Race and Sports Book.

Shopping: Stroll along the Boulevard (indoors) and find many up-scale French-style shops. Every man's man knows the value of a good cigar, and at Cigar du Monde you will be lighting only the best smokes from Honduras and the Dominican Republic. The staff is very knowledgeable and will help as you navigate the huge selection of stogies. Want some French bling-bling? I recommend the Clio Blue jewelers. This store carries the finest European jewelry in all of Vegas. If you were lucky at the tables, pick up a stylish watch from their fine selection. When you go back home, you'll be the only one out of your buddies with a unique timepiece.

New York, New York

First Opened: 1997

Ambiance: The Big Apple in the big desert.

Main Attraction: The New York City skyline and Manhattan Express roller coaster.

Location: 3970 Las Vegas Blvd. South (across the street from the MGM Grand, next to the Monte Carlo Resort & Casino).

Contact Info: 888-693-6763, www.nynyhotelcasino.com

Resting Your Head: A man's man stays in the Players Suite at this hip hotel, which is typically 800 square feet and has a Jacuzzi shaped like a four-leaf clover. Now that's what I call a good-luck soak! For approximately $200 a night, this is one of the best values in all of Las Vegas. (Sometimes a man's man likes to keep a little in his pocket so he has more cash to use at the tables.) Another option for a man's man is the Marquis Suite. As you walk into your room, you're welcomed by a marble tile entryway—a plush bed and relaxing hot tub also await you. With 700 square feet at your disposal, there's a decent amount of room to pre-game with some drinks with your fellow men's men before you head out on the town.

Recover: The New York, New York spa is open daily from 6:30 A.M. until 7:00 P.M. If you're getting the urge for an afternoon cocktail, there's a guilt-free option at the New York, New York spa: the Margarita Salt Scrub body treatment. The scrub (costing $100) uses sea salt with lemon and lime. After the therapist uses the mixture on your skin, he or she removes the salt with a warm shower. Then, he or she rubs lotion all over your skin—every man's man knows that the ladies like smooth skin. So even if it's something you wouldn't normally do, give it a try and you'll be pleasantly surprised. The spa also offers something called a "Gentlemen's Facial." Now, this name really struck a chord with me, so I decided to give it a try. The steam made me forget just for a moment that my trip was ending soon. It was very relaxing and worth the $105 tab (and my wife couldn't stop kissing my face the whole flight home!). If you want to unwind by the pool with a drink and your favorite read, look no further than the Park Avenue poolside area. This pool locale has just been upgraded for 2005, and now features cabana reservations. The sound system here is pretty impressive, and there is also an outdoor dining area where you can grab a light lunch with your date or your man's man crew. If you want to unwind further, there's even a poolside chair massage offered. It is a very different experience to be in this New York, New York setting, at a pool surrounded by skyscrapers, but, hey, anything goes in Vegas. The New York, New York Hotel & Casino strongly recommends visiting the Primm Valley Golf Course. So, after you put on one of your new golf shirts, head on over with the guys to one of two spectacular Tom Fazio–designed golf courses: the Lakes course and the Desert course. These courses were honored as two of the top 100 public courses in the nation on *Golf Magazine*'s prestigious "Top 100 You Can Play" list for the year 2000. The Lakes course, which has appeared on the list in previous years, was ranked fifty-first, and the Desert course debuted at ninety-three. After a day on the course in the heat, you can head over to the clubhouse, which has a posh locker room and showers. Now, get cleaned up and go to the dining room and bar for a great meal and a few refreshing drinks. What a man's man day!

Dining/Entertainment: If you have ever been to New York City, you know that Gallagher's Steakhouse is a great place to get an excellent steak. Well, you're in luck, because at the New York, New York Hotel & Casino, there's a Gallagher's on the premises. This place serves fresh seafood and the finest steaks around. Make sure you call for a reservation because this restaurant is extremely popular. At Il Fornaio, you can get some tasty Northern Italian meals. Choose from the wood-fired rotisserie chicken and duck, homemade and imported pasta, mesquite grilled fish, steak, and chops. My favorite is the pizza from the wood-burning oven. Also the restaurant's pastries and Italian coffees are sure to satisfy your need for something sweet along with a tasty beverage to balance it out. A man's man watches his physique, but once in a while he can indulge. At the ESPN Zone there are some really cute waitresses, but that's not what you are really there to watch—with more than 165 television monitors throughout the 33,000-square-foot facility, you won't miss a moment of your favorite games. Ever wonder how a bartender can pour those drinks so quickly and with such ease? Well, at Coyote Ugly you can get a close-up look at how it's really done, Wild West style. At this joint, you can really let loose. Sometimes even the most refined man's man has to get wild. Your lady can even dance up on the bar! The waitresses really get you into the party mode. You can't talk about New York, New York, without talking about the hotel's hard-core roller coaster called the Manhattan Express. Can you say "very adventurous" at 67 mph? Well, a man has to prove a thing or two once in a while, so you have to try this fast and rather intense ride. With heights of 203 feet and drops of 144 feet, this ride will definitely knock the gel right out of your hair. If an adrenaline rush is what you're looking for, look no further. No time for wimping out—the Manhattan Express roller coaster separates the men from the boys.

Gaming: New York, New York has an 84,000-square-foot casino. What a place! The highlight of the New York, New York gaming experience is the new Asian "Dragon Pit." The Asian-influenced gaming area offers mini-baccarat, Sic Bo, three-card poker, and pai gow poker. With more than eighty gaming tables and over 2,000 slot machines, this is definitely a man's man gambling experience. Something for everyone!

Shopping: This might not be the actual New York City shopping experience, but it is one of the best places to spend some cash in Vegas. Go to the SoHo Village for a cool downtown vibe. You'll really feel like you're in the Big Apple. Every man's man knows that a quality timepiece is tops on the list. So, if you hit it big at the tables, go to the Grand Central Watch Company. This store carries Raymond Weil and other top brands. Just in case you're visiting Vegas to celebrate a special occasion, they also have some pretty diamond necklaces for the ladies. For a laugh you might want to buy something at the I Love New York, New York Signature Shop, with over 2,000 items with the "NY" logo on it. There's something cool you can select for just about anyone. Want to play a joke on one of your buddies? At Houdini's Magic Shop, there are a lot of funny gags and tricks. Maybe the guys you are sharing your suite with are getting on your nerves. A man's man knows when a joke is needed to ease the tension. Hey, watch out, roommate. Here comes trouble!

* * *

Man's Man
Interview with
James Caan

New York City native James Caan, who studied acting at the prestigious Neighborhood Playhouse, has been electrifying movie and
television screens with his man's man persona for decades. He played
the unforgettable part of Sonny Corleone in Francis Ford Coppola's
epic mafia movie *The Godfather*. Caan's diversity as an actor is as-
tounding. For instance, he played a cowboy in films like *Comes A
Horseman* (1978) and *Another Man, Another Chance* (1977), a compul-
sive gambler in the film *The Gambler* (1974), a tough guy in the film
Thief (1981), and even a best-selling author in the hit movie *Misery*
(1990), where he starred opposite Kathy Bates. Caan has appeared
opposite some of the most dynamic female co-stars in the business,
including Barbra Streisand (*Funny Lady*), Halle Berry (*The Program*),
and Charlize Theron (*The Yards*), just to name a few. Caan is also no
stranger to Las Vegas—in fact, he has been going to the desert
hotspot for business and pleasure for many, many years. He appeared
in the hit comedy film *Honeymoon in Vegas* (shot on location in Vegas)

and, most recently, he's starring in the hit television drama series aptly entitled *Las Vegas*. James Caan is a man's man who has seen all the ins and outs of Sin City. So, listen up . . .

Frank Vincent: *Do you remember the first time you went to Las Vegas?*

James Caan: I was in my early to mid twenties. I started riding horses, and one of my friends was one of the small owners of Caesar's. This was way before Caesar's went corporate. So, I went out there to ride horses and act like a cowboy from New York. I was a brash little wiseguy kid and had all my "New York stuff" in me. I spent most of my time in those days at Caesar's and the Sands. I became friendly with a lot of the guys out there.

FV: *Coming from New York, how did you feel about the desert?*

JC: I hate the desert. Who wants to take a cactus out of your ass (laughing).

FV: *(Laughing) I hear you. What about the excitement of Las Vegas?*

JC: Seriously, at that age there was always something exciting to do in Las Vegas, especially when you knew some of the upper echelon hotel owners. Also, as a young kid, the girls were phenomenal. But, it was far removed from the way it is today. Today, it is all corporate. Back then, if you were a friend, you got the pencil (comped), which was the biggest gift in the world if you were a young guy. I used to hang out with and watch comedians like Don Adams, Shecky Greene, and Don Rickles perform.

FV: *Who are some of the other entertainers you've seen perform in Vegas?*

JC: There was Frank Sinatra, of course. We had some mutual friends. I went to his house and got to know him fairly well. Sinatra had seen a picture I did in 1969 called *The Rain People* and he wanted to talk about that. So, I spent a whole night with him. As far as other entertainers, I loved watching Louis Prima. Also, for pure entertainment, I loved watching Steve Lawrence and Edie Gorme. They always offered great music and a lot of laughs. They were classic Vegas entertainment at its best. Shecky Greene was hilarious. If you went to see him every night, you *always* saw a different show. You never saw the same show twice.

FV: *Shecky was pure thunder. What about Dean Martin?*

JC: Oh, Dean was one of my best friends for years. He was a great performer. He was also a cowboy, and one of my biggest influences. I used to practice out at his ranch all the time. Then, I joined the PRCA (Professional Rodeo Cowboy Association).

FV: *One of my biggest dreams is to play a cowboy in a movie. I tell my wife that every day because Dean was one of my heroes.*

JC: Yes, Dean was a pretty good cowboy. Rodeo was a big sport and we all used to hang out at Dean's ranch. As a matter a fact, I got married to my son Scott's mother at Dean's ranch and the ceremony was on horseback. At the time, Kirk Kerkorian gave me his suite at the MGM as a wedding gift. My earliest memories of Las Vegas are all of fun times. Of course, I didn't have any money back then. I once owed $12,000 and, at the time, I thought that was four years' work (laughing)!

FV: *(Laughing) You starred in the 1974 movie* **The Gambler.** *Have you always been intrigued by gambling?*

JC: My father played a lot of gin rummy and had a system with the horses, which was hysterical. He and his cousin, who was a stockbroker, had files and files for this system in order to follow the horses. So, I was around gambling from an early age. I remember that they were playing gin games in the back of the local barbershop, with a curtain drawn to cover the action.

FV: *In my old neighborhood, the gambling took place in a taxicab office.*

JC: Well, our spot was the local barbershop. It was hysterical because they had this little curtain that barely covered the opening to the back room and there were six guys behind it playing three across. The barbershop owner would keep screaming at them to be quiet and to keep it down. He would tell them every day that

---

JAMES CAAN

Favorite Man's Man Game:
Blackjack

Favorite Man's Man Drink to Have While Gambling:
Vodka on the rocks

Favorite Man's Man Restaurant in Vegas:
Prime (at the Bellagio)

Favorite Man's Man Golf Course:
Shadow Creek

Favorite Man's Man Entertainer to Perform in Vegas:
Frank Sinatra

---

this was the last time they could ever play again because they were chasing his customers away. But, he never closed it. However, when I was young, my father once told me, "The only time you should gamble is when you've got nothing."

FV: *Exactly right. That's good.*

JC: I always remembered that piece of advice. Obviously, when you lost, what did you really lose? Because you still had nothing. When you've got money and you're making money gambling, like $5,000 or $10,000, it's not going to change your life. It's only going to aggravate you if you lose. I believe that's true, because I am a terrible loser at anything I play. I will gamble a little bit now, but I stopped really enjoying it. I don't get thrilled by gambling now.

FV: *What do you like to play, if you are going to gamble?*

JC: I enjoy playing blackjack, because I have a system in a book (laughing).

FV: *(Laughing) Will you give me the book?*

JC: I'll give you the whole book, Frank. (Laughing) Blackjack is all about money management, like any game. My mother, your mother, and anybody else who gambles in Las Vegas who is *not* a real gambler is how those places get built out there. Also, the people who think they are gamblers are full of crap. There are maybe one-tenth of 1 percent of people who are true gamblers. You've got to have ice water in your veins to be a genuine gambler. For example, my friends or my mother will go to Vegas and go with $2,000. They'll say, "I'm going to go with $2,000 and if I lose it, so what? I am going to have a good time." That's what they all say! The money varies with each person. If they are losing $5,000, they'll usually end up spending $20,000 to get even. You can hear them out loud at the tables saying, "Oh please, let me get even!" Right Frank?

FV: *Absolutely.*

JC: Now, if they are betting with $5,000 and winning, what do they say? They say, "I am going to go home with at least $2,500 in winnings." How are they going to hurt the hotel with that attitude? Every person has this in common. Even if a person is winning $2,000, he or she is ready to settle for $1,000 in winnings in order to go home a winner. However, if someone wants to get even, they will spend $10,000 to get even. Now, the cold-blooded gambler does the exact opposite. When he's winning, his thought process is that it ain't his money. It's the casino's money. So, he bets it all. When he is losing, he cuts down. It sounds simple, but it is *very* hard to do.

FV: *You starred in many films shot in Sin City, including* **Honeymoon in Vegas** *in 1992. Coming full circle, you're now the star of the hit TV show* **Las Vegas.** *Did you ever think you would be on a network television show shot there?*

JC: No, and I still don't believe it. I had a lot of reasons for doing it. I have two young kids. With all the movies being shot in Canada these days, my kids wouldn't be able to visit me as much. I basically decided to do a network television show so I could stay home. The truth is that I get up before they go to school and I come home after they go to bed. So, we'll see where that goes.

FV: *How has Vegas changed in your eyes over the years?*

JC: Well, it's very corporate now. Traditionally, in the old days, friends of the bosses got breaks, comps, etc. Today, everything is according to how much time you spend at the table, how much time you spend there when you're winning, how much time you spend at the table when you're losing, your average bet, etc. There are all kinds of criteria that constitute you getting a comp. It has nothing to do with who you know, it has to do with your play, how you play, and how much time you play. That's it! In my eyes, it has become very impersonal.

FV: *Computers took over.*

JC: Yes. They know every single thing. If they catch you in that "eye in the sky" just looking weird, you're gone from the casino!

FV: *I know you love boxing, Jimmy. What are some of the most memorable fights you've seen live in Vegas?*

JC: There have been so many good fights over the years. My wife and I were there for the Mike Tyson vs. Evander Holyfield ear biting incident. Half of Brooklyn was there for the Vito Enterfurmo/Marvin Hagler fight, and it was the same night Benetez and Sugar Ray Leonard fought. I remember seeing Trinidad's first fight there. I saw the final fight for Sylvester Stallone's boxing TV show, *The Contender.* It was really great. I continue to go to good fights in Las Vegas.

FV: *What do you do during your downtime in Las Vegas?*

JC: I recently looked at my birth certificate and started playing golf.

FV: *(Laughing) You've worked in and traveled to many man's man destinations all over the world. Does Vegas throw off something special for you when you step off the plane?*

JC: Yeah, heat!

FV: *(Laughing) We'll end on that note, Jimmy. You're a man's man all the way.*

JC: Thanks. So are you, Frank.

**Looking
Like a Man's Man**

Everyone knows that women like men who have it all together, who look clean and sharp. Hey, not all of us resemble James Bond, but if you put yourself together properly, you can be as appealing as him. (Well, almost!) Life is about presentation. People go for the sizzle and then the steak . . . know what I mean? What is a Christmas gift without the gift wrap and bow? What is that great Italian dish without the sauce and fresh basil? What is the martini without the olives? You get it now. With a line wrapped around the block at a "hot" club with a bunch of "ham and eggers" chomping at the bit to get in, you want to be the one noticed at the door wearing your sharp leather coat and your shined shoes, and walk in VIP style. You want to be the one at the gym who all the ladies are diggin', even if your pecs aren't perfect. You want to be the one at the family wedding in the best custom tux, looking even better than the groom. You might not have been the one chosen as the best man, but you might as well be the *best-dressed* man, right?

In this chapter, I am also going to discuss the do's and don'ts in the attire department. A man's man also learns from mistakes. This past summer, I was in the supermarket and a fan passed me in one of the aisles and said, "Frank, I love your work." I thanked him and we parted ways. About five minutes later, he passed me again and asked, "Are you shooting *Sopranos* right now?" I replied, "Yes." He said, "Whatever you do, don't wear those shorts on *Sopranos* with those skinny legs!" I had a good laugh and never wore those shorts again.

One thing is for sure, women love a man who smells and looks good. The characters I have played during my career have always dressed well. For instance, Salvy from *Raging Bull* was in a pinstripe suit, a long collar, white-on-white shirt with initials on the cuff, and shoes so pointy they could kill cockroaches in the corner. Salvy was charming, impressive, and a true ladies' man. It's always fun to dress up for period piece movies—*Raging Bull* ('50s), *Goodfellas* ('60s), *Casino* ('70s), *Gotti* ('80s), etc.

Bottom line, fellas, you can talk like a man's man and walk like a man's man, but without the right look, you're not the complete package. Take some notes on the things you wouldn't catch a man's man dead wearing:

- Anything from a "buy one, get one free rack"
- Anything made out of 100 percent polyester
- Any item that's been in your closet for more than two years
- Any T-shirts with juvenile sayings like: MY GIRLFRIEND'S OUT OF TOWN
- Anything ruffled
- Anything your great-aunt gave you for Christmas
- A piano tie
- A Speedo

Now, I'm going to make it easy on you by letting you know all the gear that a man's man should have in his possession. That includes clothing, shoes, ties, accessories, grooming products, and even cars. Yeah, I said cars. When you pull up to your date's place of residence and you are dressed to the nines, you need to have the car to go with the look. No Dodge Darts here, boys. Leave that heap at home and rent a car if you must. Or work your ass off, put in overtime, and get the right ride. Okay, buckle up, here we go!

The Looks

The Formal Look

THE BREAKDOWN

Right off the bat, I've got to state my claim: a true man doesn't rent a tuxedo. There are exceptions to the rule: For instance, if you just landed in Florida for a wedding and the airline lost your luggage, then you're renting, pal. But, as a rule, a man's man should have at least one tuxedo, tailored to perfection, at his fingertips. Since he's a "man about town," he never knows when he'll get a last-minute call for a first-class event. There have been times when at the last minute I've been invited to a *Sopranos* event and when I pulled my tuxedo out of the closet, it looked as clean and crisp as the day I bought it. So, you should be prepared at all times with your tuxedo and shirt ready to wear. *What designers should you buy?* A man's man buys whatever he can afford. If you like and can afford a Giorgio Armani (approx.

$1,850) tuxedo, then by all means go for it. Armani makes beautiful things. If that is out of your price range, you're not any less of a man. A man's man will find a nice tuxedo and get it fitted right. If it doesn't fit properly, at the next party someone might ask you for shrimp puffs. That's not what a man's man wants to hear. One last thing: It's not just about the look, it's also about the attitude when you're wearing it. Confidence!

Foot Gear: Patent leather shoes are out. A man's man knows that a quality pair of black leather shoes is a wise investment. You want to buy shoes that are comfortable. With supple, shiny-leather footwear, you're sure to get noticed!

Where to Wear It: If you get an invitation in the mail and it reads, BLACK TIE, then you've got to throw your tuxedo on. Also, if you're nominated for an award (Oscar, Grammy, Emmy, Best Dog in Show) a tuxedo is the right thing to wear. However, if you wear a tux to an event that does not have BLACK TIE on the invite, someone might ask you to bring their car around front. Please use discretion and only wear a tuxedo when it's called for—formal weddings, benefits, awards dinners, etc.

Accents: *Bow tie or regular tie, that is the question.* A man's man goes regular tie with a tuxedo. The bow tie is definitely out of date. I can't stress it enough that you do not want to look like a headwaiter or a maître 'd. If you watch awards shows, you'll hardly ever see stars wearing bow ties. A handkerchief that matches the tie is always a nice addition.

By the way, a man's man does not actually use it to blow his nose. If it's allergy season, bring some back-up tissues. A handkerchief is for accent use only. Cuff links are also a smart purchase because they can be worn with your regular suits as well. Remember, "people in the know" tend to look at that stuff. It could help you strike up a conversation at a wedding with one of the bride's gorgeous cousins from out of town. Wedding + cousin from out of town = one wild night!

The Workout Look

THE BREAKDOWN

If you think the workout attire of a man's man consists of some sweats and an armpit-stained T-shirt picked up in the parking lot of a Van Halen concert back in '86, think again. A real man's man wears quality athletic attire that's stylish. For instance, Puma, New Balance, and Nike make great athletic apparel. Also, there's a difference between athletic pants and sweatpants. Athletic pants are like the ones I'm wearing in the picture (stripe down the leg, made of nylon/cotton material), but sweatpants are something to be worn when you take out the garbage at six in the morning with a hangover. Also, a man's man does not bring his own towel to the gym. He belongs to a first-rate heath club that supplies fresh towels for all of its clientele. After a man's man pumps some iron on the bench, he wipes it down with his towel so the next guy ain't working out in a pool of his sweat. That's the proper protocol. A gym bag is important because a man's man does not just walk into the health club like a slob holding newspapers, magazines, water bottles, and a change of clothes. He goes in there with his bag and a lock for his locker. Also, you should always wears white socks—not girlie tennis socks with pom poms or barefeet underneath your sneaks. Nothing is more offensive than a guy doing crunches next to you with stinky feet. No black dress socks, either. Also, no undershirts with pizza stains. A man's man can be tastefully sleeveless, but he does not buy any tanks that are sold in a three-pack for $2. None of that cheap nonsense allowed! At a health club, you could meet business contacts, friends, and, most important, future dates. So, "never let them see you sweat" too much! P.S. Have your hairy back waxed, and no grunting like a farm animal when you're lifting heavy weights.

Where to Wear It: Too many guys try the "sweatsuit mob look," and that's on its way out, big time! Unless, you're under the age of fifteen, heading to a tryout for the next boy band, or appearing on *The Sopranos*, you don't wear athletic gear un-less you plan on being athletic. Know what I'm saying? Your workout look is good for places like the gym, playing basketball, bike riding, or jogging in the park with your dog (which is also a great chick magnet). I don't care what you say, fellas, a cute puppy beats out big biceps any day of the week. Also, you could wear your workout clothes when you play a little tennis with your lovely lady. A man's man does not wear an all-white tight tennis outfit when he plays—that's for wimps!

Accents: Good triceps!

Foot Gear: If you think that when a man's man goes to the gym, he just throws on some ratty old tennis shoes that he wears when he mows the lawn on Saturdays, think again. A man's man wears a good pair of name-brand sneakers with clean laces. If you're buying your sneakers from a bin, you got problems. If you're buying your sneakers in an aisle that also sells breakfast cereal, you got bigger problems. Also a man's man buys a new pair of sneakers every six months. If yours still look good after six months, then you're not exercising enough. P.S. No Velcro allowed!

The Sleek Suit Look

THE BREAKDOWN

A man's man should always make sure his suits are of superior quality. I am not talking about off the rack, either, unless you're a man's man in training or a pimple-faced sixteen-year old going to a bar mitzvah. If neither of those apply, then you need to get your suits handmade (preferably by an Italian). Always go custom, guys. If you really can't afford it, buy off the rack—just make sure your suit is tailored properly. Now, the most flattering pants are flat front trousers. No pleats, gentlemen. Unless you're Woody Allen, tweed ain't the ticket either. He's the only one who can pull that off and not be on a "worst-dressed list." Don't worry. You don't have to spend a mint on the suit. Also, a custom shirt is always the way to go. Getting a custom suit without a custom shirt is like getting a Range Rover without the navigation system. No skimping here. When picking a custom shirt from a clothier, be certain to choose a fabric and color that coordinates nicely with your suit. Also, it's all about the mix and match. So, pick items that can be worn in a few different combinations. Getting your shirt monogrammed with your initials is a nice touch, too. The initials go on the cuff or on the pocket. That's the hip way to do it.

Where to Wear It: Fancy dinner dates, movie premieres, job interviews, meetings, power lunches with the guys, Broadway shows, benefits, funerals (a man's man always pays his respects). Fellas, take your date somewhere nice so you can show off your duds, but don't be afraid to wear this look anywhere you need to to look dapper and cool.

Accents: A great custom suit always requires a fabulous silk tie. Fellas, not having the right tie can be the deal breaker in many situations! If you have problems putting together the suit, shirt, and tie, ask someone for help. Ask a nice-looking woman friend; ask the guy who is selling and taking the measurements for your suit; consult your gay neighbor in apt 3B; ask who you must, but please, get the right tie. I have heard many horror stories of men getting turned down by women or not getting the job because of the tie they wore. Most important thing to remember: always pick a silk tie. No ties from New York City street vendors—if it is not the *real* Louis Vuitton, please do not wear it. Also, a handkerchief in your front suit pocket is very stylish. *Note: It doesn't have to match your tie.* A little color contrast works in this case. Wear a "hot" watch (by "hot" I mean in style, not from some guy whose idea of a showroom is the inside lining of his trench coat). A name-brand watch is a mainstay. So, put in overtime, get a new job, but get a great watch. If the sun is in your eyes or you just want to look cool, a nice pair of shades completes this look. If you are headed out for a lunch meeting, try some Coach shades, which are classic and cool.

Foot Gear: Again, black leather shoes. There are many styles to choose from: wing-tip, lace-up, loafer, ornamented with silver buckle. The only way you'll lose is if they are not shined and clean. If you dare to wear sandals with a suit (and I don't care if they are Italian leather), you should be shot! The only man's man who could get away with open-toe sandals was Jesus. Hey, I know a guy likes to save a buck here and there, but if you're into Payless shoes, then you must be into Band-Aids because they are blister city. Payless is not a part of the man's man vocabulary. Buy one, get one free? That's weak talk!

The Nightclub Look

THE BREAKDOWN

Unless you're Bruce Willis, chances are you ain't getting into a hot nightclub in a major city wearing jeans. I know what you're saying, "But Frank, I only wear Diesel and Versace jeans!" Yeah, yeah, yeah, but trust me. You'll have better luck getting past the doorman if you show up wearing a nice pair of slacks. Of course, all black is the safe way to go when going to a nightclub, but a man's man tries to mix it up. He'll combine a nice black leather jacket (an Andrew Marc leather coat is the way to go) with a nice stylish shirt (Hugo Boss, Zegna, Ralph Lauren, Tommy Hillfiger are all good choices). When the ladies in the nightclub see that you treat yourself right with some good attire, they know you'll treat them right.

Where to Wear It: You want to wear this to a hot club with a tough door policy. You want to get the VIP treatment, and this outfit screams, "bottle service."

Accents: A good cologne at a nightclub is *always* a must. Wear a scent that complements you—nice enough to get the ladies attracted, but not so strong that they get turned off. I guarantee inquiring female minds will want to know your phone number. A money clip, especially one from Tiffany, is definitely the way to go. You do not want a big wallet, with receipts and crap sticking out of it, adding unwanted pounds to your rear section. Also, the Tiffany Valet key ring is important when going to a club in a place like Los Angeles (where valet service is everywhere). The Valet key ring is a double-sided key ring, which lets you take your house keys with you. Hey, there are some shady people out there, and a man's man makes sure his stuff is safe at all times. When at a club and exchanging numbers with a business contact or an attractive female, having the right business-card in the right business-card holder is essential. Spring for the upgraded business card with the fancy lettering. A Coach belt is also a nice move. Make sure it matches your shoes, and you're all set.

Foot Gear: It really depends on the club. If you are going with your friends to a lounge or bar with a non-strict door policy, I suggest Cole Haan, Coach, Kenneth Cole, or Steve Madden. If you're going to a hot nightclub harder to get into than the White House, I suggest Prada boots in the fall/winter and Gucci loafers in the

spring/summer. If you are going to an Irish pub to throw back a couple of pints of Guinness (a man's man *only* drinks imported beer), then put on some Diesel sneakers and you'll be relaxed and looking good.

Getting Past the Doorman

G uys often have problems getting into the hot nightclub of the moment. Nothing is more embarrassing than having the door-man tell you those fatal four words, "Sorry, guest list only." Hey, we all dream of getting the treatment that Henry Hill (Ray Liotta) received when he entered the Copacabana nightclub in *Goodfellas*. Well, a man's man not only gets past the doorman, he gets the VIP treatment the whole night through. I called upon a friend of mine, King, who just so happens to be a doorman at some of the hottest nightclubs in New York City, for some inside information. (By the way, King is a man's man name if I ever heard one!) For the last decade, King has worked the door at top places like Spa, Limelight, Life, and NA. These clubs cater to celebrities as well as a mix of downtown and Upper East Side Manhattanites. You have to be a man's man to get into one of these hot spots, and the one who makes the final decision of whether to lift the velvet rope or give you rope burn is the doorman. I can tell you this: If you don't look like a man's man, you won't be popping bottles in one of these clubs; you'll be popping a Snapple from the deli on the corner.

I stopped by NA to get *you* some advice on how to get in the door, and to get *myself* a martini with three olives. Let's hear what King has to say . . .

Frank Vincent: *King, what's happening, man?*

King: Good to see you, Frank.

FV: *So, you've worked at some of the hottest clubs in all of Manhattan. Who are some men's men you've opened the velvet rope for?*

K: Denzel Washington, Derek Jeter, Stevie Wonder, Tommy Lee, just to name few. I also have to mention some of the lovely ladies who have stopped by like Heather Graham, Paris Hilton, Lindsey Lohan, and Pamela Anderson.

FV: *That's some good clientele. King, what advice can you give someone who wants to get into your club?*

In the words of Mötley Crüe, "Girls, Girls, Girls." Bring your neighbor, cousin, sister, or some women from a random bachelorette party you happen to stumble upon. The only thing more impressive to a doorman than a guy with five girls is a guy with six girls. You don't have to be sleeping with them, just show up with them. Other women are sure to be impressed by that. The other thing I suggest is to follow my three F's: Funky, Fabulous, and Fashionable. Nice shoes, a fat money clip, and a flashy business card can also help. The big no-no is a white limo. It wasn't even cool when you were at your high school prom. Lastly, one should never ask, "Don't you know who I am?"

FV: *(Laughing) That's solid advice. How about tipping?*

K: Even that can be presented in the wrong way. A man's man does not hang his tip out there for all eyes to see. He also does not say things out loud like, *"How much does it cost me to get in?"* A man's man does his business casually—like it is something he would normally do.

FV: *I agree that a man's man is* **always** *discreet about his business.*

K: Yes. He is discreet, well-groomed and, above all, confident about himself. I remember I turned down some guy who tried to give me $500.

FV: *Why, because he didn't look like a man's man?*

K: Exactly. The guy had his shirt open and twenty gold chains on. The only guy I would let into my club with twenty gold chains is Mr. T. Also, approach the velvet rope of my club, or any club for that matter, dressed like you belong in a nightclub, not looking like you belong in a gymnasium.

FV: *Nowadays, baseball caps seem to be popular and are being worn at the clubs. That does not represent a man's man to me.*

K: People wearing baseball caps are generally the people I don't let into the club. Now, some celebrities come to my club wearing hats, but they can do whatever they want. I also want to say that being well groomed, confident, and well-put-together doesn't mean you have to be wearing a suit. James Dean wore a T-shirt and jeans and he looked like a superstar at all times. That's because it was his look and, most important, he wore it confidently. Nowadays, these kids are wearing whatever looks good on people on MTV and a big style in the hip-hop world is an oversized white T-shirt with the gold "bling-bling."

That doesn't present style to me. You might get into some club looking like that. But you won't get in a club that's exclusive, and that's only where a man's man goes.

FV: *Well, we've got to keep in mind that man's man Hugh Hefner wears pajamas to nightclubs.*

K: Well, I think pajamas are cool. I have even worked the door in pajamas.

FV: *Six gorgeous Playmates on his arm doesn't hurt either.*

K: I believe six Playmates is the ultimate "all in" in poker. That's definitely not a bluff. Anybody who can bring six Playmates to a nightclub can forget about having to tip anyone.

FV: *Okay, here's the scenario. A guy approaches your club on a busy night, with a hundred people waiting. Half are girls wearing almost nothing, so it's tough to get noticed. What should a guy look like to get your attention?*

K: Well, for openers, I could pick you out of the crowd because you are the most crazily dressed person in the world and I might want one of those types in there. But, if you are crazily dressed and it doesn't look like your own personal style, then it won't work. Everyone says to dress in all black if you do not know the doorman, and that isn't a bad idea. A great jacket like the one you're wearing, Frank, would be perfect. The leather on that jacket looks like it's worth more than some of the cars parked on this block. Now, if you're from Miami and you're trying to get into a New York club and you're dressing in Miami style, it's probably not going to cut it either.

FV: *If you see some guy coming up to the door who's obviously not of man's man caliber, how do you tell him to "Hit the road, Jack?"*

K: I don't like to be mean to people at first. I might say something like, "This is a private event and if you're not on the guest list, I can't help you." We try not to be like the notorious Steve Rubell at Studio 54 who bluntly told people things like, "How dare you show up at my club dressed like that?" We generally want people in the club who look good and spend even better.

FV: *How can you tell if some random guy is a spender or a hanger-on?*

K: The first thing every doorman learns is to look at people's shoes to see if they have money. Listen, we have bottle service at our club starting at a $300 minimum. That's not cheap. So, we cater to a certain level of clientele. However, if you have money, but are acting like an asshole, that doesn't mean I am going to let you in either. I had two guys, and I'm not going to name names, who are known killers who approached the door. They told me they were going to kill me if I didn't let them in the club. I didn't let them in, and they didn't kill me.

FV: *Sticking by your guns; I respect that. You're a man's man doorman if I've ever heard of one.*

K: Any good doorman will tell you that it's *not* based 100 percent on money. There are moments when conversation can come into play. If a guy comes up, looks you in the eye, smiles right, and seems like a person who is going to go in and have a good time and not cause problems, then I will probably let them in. Sometimes they say the right things and seem nice. Hey, a man's man has to look good and talk well.

FV: *I agree that a man's man has to walk the walk as well as talk the talk. Does a man's man always* **have** *to get bottle service at a nightclub?*

K: A man's man does not need to show off. He gets a table and bottle if it's appropriate. My advice is that if a man's man shows up at the club with a date, he should get a table in a dark corner of the club. However, if he's celebrating after a great day at the track with the guys, he pops bottles at a table out in the open. But, he's also confident enough that he doesn't have to buy bottles of Cristal and spray them on the floor. Again, a true man's man is one who does not need to show off, but can when he wants to. Like man's man author Mark Twain once said, "It's not bragging if you can back it up."

Grooming

A man's man can be dressed in one of the sharpest suits imaginable, but if he's got nose or ear hair so long it could be braided, it's sure to kill the look. A nicely pressed shirt and a pair of well-shined shoes without a clean shave and a good haircut is like a Benz without the engine. Do yourself a favor, and be complete with your look. You should shave a minimum of every other day and do an overall maintenance (fingernails, toenails, sideburns, etc.) a minimum of once a week. You've got to take the time to go over your appearance. Even a little goes a long way. As I mentioned in the introduction to this book, my father always smelled and looked great. When I was a young boy, I would often watch my dad get dressed. He would take the time to make sure that his appearance was as polished as his shoes. When he walked into a room, he had an air, a presence about him that would make people stop and take notice. He showed me from an early age that when you are groomed correctly, people will definitely take you more seriously in business and life. First impressions are everything. You need a little guidance in the grooming department? Read my advice, and you'll be off to the races.

The Haircut

Choosing the right barber is like choosing the right numbers in roulette. If you choose correctly, you'll come out a big winner. Choose incorrectly, and you go home a loser (not to mention wearing a hat for the next eight weeks). The haircut is a major part of your look and appeal. You need someone who is going to cut your hair in a stylish and age-appropriate way. Plus, don't forget "year-appropriate." The long, shabby, wild hairstyle might have been cool back in the '70s, but not now, fellas. As far as hairstyles from the '80s are concerned, a man's man forgets that decade ever existed. He doesn't use a buzzer on his own head or a bowl from his breakfast cereal to cut his hair. (If you're forty-five years old and your mother still cuts your hair, you've got more problems than a math book.) Also, unless you're Fabio, or Furio from *The Sopranos*, ponytails are out. You need to go to a barber who knows your lifestyle, knows what looks good on you and knows what's hip.

Now, a man's man goes to a *real* barbershop—a local place where everybody knows your name when you walk in. "Hey, Frank, how you been, pal? How's your family?" That's the warm treatment a man's man should receive. He doesn't go into some fancy schmantzy beauty salon and read *Cosmopolitan* magazine while surrounded by twenty women with more tinfoil in their hair than what's used to cover a honey-glazed ham baking in the oven. No, a man's man goes to the barbershop and talks politics, sports, music, and movies. He knows his barber by name and they have a good rapport. Around the holidays, he brings his barber a bottle of red wine as a gift. Are you catching my drift? Here's the bottom line: You want to have a good rapport and friendship with anybody who's using a scissor and straight-edge razor on your face and neck.

Here are some surefire signs that you're not in a man's man barbershop:

- They ask you to sweep up your own hair after the cut.

- Your hairdresser Ramon begins to massage you, but it's not on the menu of services.

- Your barber ingests a shot of Barbicide before he begins your straight razor shave.

- The health inspection sign dates back to the Ford administration.

- The scissor is rustier than an '82 Chevy Malibu.

- They offer dog grooming under the same roof.

If you don't have hair, it's not the end of the world. Remember, a man's man works with what he has. In fact, there are many men's men who are bald and wear it extremely well. Actors like Sean Connery, Ed Harris, and Vin Diesel all look good. Don't wear a rug, especially not a cheap one. In this day and age, going natural is the best ticket.

Chest hair is a tricky situation. If you don't have any, it's not a problem. If you do have chest hair, it could be a problem if you let it grow like ragweed. You need to keep it in check. In many European countries, the men let their chest hair grow naturally. So what? Many women in those same European countries let their underarm hair grow naturally. What does that tell you? Letting your chest hair run its course is definitely out of the question. So, what's the desired limit on length? I was home one night and my wife, Kathy, had a couple of girlfriends over. They were all watching that movie *The Thomas Crown Affair* starring Pierce Brosnan. There was a scene when Pierce had his shirt off, and they commented on how nice his chest hair looked. Well, that's your guideline, fellas—Pierce Brosnan's chest hair! His is trimmed right, and women like it. Hey, women don't want to date Chewbacca from *Star Wars*, they want Han Solo. So, groom yourself. If you're embarrassed, just keep it on the down low. Also, please note that if you have chest hair popping out of the top of your shirt, take care of it immediately. Back hair? Please! That doesn't even exist in a man's mans world. In horror movies haven't you noticed all the gorgeous women *run away* from werewolves?

Manicure/Pedicure

A man's man *does* get a manicure. He is confident enough in his sexuality to do so. I am not saying to get French tips—just a cut, file, and buff, and you're ready to rock. Are you a little skeptical about getting a manicure? Well, even tough guys get them. Don't believe me? Early in my career, I was involved in a booking agency where I booked musical talent. I knew all the club owners. One particular owner, who you might say was "connected," called me in one afternoon because he wanted to hire some talent I represented. When I entered the club, I was surprised (to say the least) that he and four of his associates were all sitting around a table doing their own nails. It felt like I had walked into a sixteen-year-old girl's pajama party. There were cotton balls, Q-tips, emery boards, clear nail polish—you name it! I tried to keep a straight face while the "boss" and I negotiated for one of my clients. "Frank, you got to do better on the price on that singer. Hey, Carmine pass me the cotton balls." It was one of the most surreal things I have ever witnessed. I couldn't believe that all these major tough guys were using nail polish and cotton balls. So, don't feel embarrassed or guilty the next time you get your nails primped. If mob guys don't feel it's for sissies, you shouldn't.

As a side note, women are attracted to men who get in touch with their softer side. I'm not saying to compare manicure tips with your date. But, hey, accidentally slicing your woman in bed with your toenails during sex ain't too cool. Some guys don't believe me when I tell them how important it is to have your feet on the up and up. It could be the difference between Friday night date or being more "home alone" than Macaulay Culkin. Don't believe what I'm sayin'? Check out this weird letter:

Dear Frank,

I was down at the New Jersey Shore for a weekend of fun in the sun. We spent all day Saturday at Jenkinson's Beach in Point Pleasant. My friends and I started talking to these girls and there was one who was really a looker, definitely girlfriend material. After a great conversation and a couple of pina coladas, I asked for her number. The next day, I gave her a call and asked her if she wanted to meet me for happy hour at a local bar. I noticed that when she was on the phone, she sounded a little distant. I asked what was wrong and she replied, "I have to be honest. Your toenails are a bit long. I think they need a cut." I was taken back by her honesty. She then said she wasn't available to go out that day, and to make a long story short, after numerous phone calls, she was not available any other day either. Where did I make my fatal mistake? Aren't pedicures for sissies? Talk to me, Frank.

Carl

* * *

Dear American Werewolf in Point Pleasant,

Carl, your "snaggle nail" ain't that much fun in the sun. A man's man never goes to the beach with his feet not looking presentable. You need to invest in getting out all last year's lint and any corns that have come your way. Just like men, women look over people's bodies from head to toe . . . nail! So, if you don't have the guts or funds to go get a pedicure, that's fine. But, at the very least, clip those claws once a week.

Frank

Shaving

A "guy" *only* goes by the three S's. "Shit, Shower, and Shave." Seriously, a man's man does a lot more than that before he heads out the front door. But he does take his shaving very seriously. He doesn't just throw gel on his face from some cheap aerosol can. Hey, aerosol puts a hole in the ozone layer, in case you haven't heard. Wake up! If he has the appropriate time and wants to pamper himself, he uses real shaving soap applied with a brush.

Honestly, the best shave you could ask for is a straight razor shave from your trusty barber. That reminds me of a joke: *The barber who shaved me was so nervous he cut me three times. After the shave he said, "Do you want your head wrapped in a hot towel." I said, "No, I will carry it home under my arm."* That joke kills me every time. Anyway, if you can't make it to your barber's, you should shave properly yourself. One of the keys to attracting women and impressing business clients is a smooth, quality shave. Did you ever see Donald Trump with a beard? How about Bill Gates with a goatee? No. They are true businessmen and they know the importance of a polished appearance. The scruffy look works for some, but not many. Look at the New York Yankees—nice and clean cut. The Red Sox look like a bunch of cavemen in uniforms. Get it together, guys.

The six stages to the perfect shave are as follows:

1. Prep: Apply warm towel to soften the skin and open the pores.

2. Apply: Take your time to apply the shaving soap with a brush all over your face, fully covering the areas that need to be shaved.

3. Shave: You should use a high-end razor for the closest shave possible. Note: A man's man *never* uses electric.

4. Rinse: Use cold water and wash off all excess cream and hair. Sounds simple, but cold water is one of the most important parts of the shave because it closes the pores.

5. Moisturize: Put a little moisturizer in the palm of your hand, rub your hands together, and then apply to the shaved area of the face. There's nothing like smooth skin!

6. Aftershave: Buy one to make the women go nuts. I recommend something with a light scent—women like that fresh and clean smell. Do not go for something that smells too strong; that's a major turnoff. You should also coordinate your aftershave with your cologne of choice.

A man's man does it right with a sterling silver shaving set. Invest wisely in your shaving tools and products. Your local chain pharmacy *will not* carry this type of high-end shaving instrument. Twenty disposable razors in a package for $1.99 doesn't cut it—literally! Head over to a major department store for the right shaving goods. Spend a little money on quality, and you'll notice a difference in how people react to you.

Most men also need to keep their nose and ear hair in check. Sharper Image sells a Turbo-Clipper ($49.95) for home use and a great travel care kit ($79.95) for the man's man on the road. Maintenance on your own sideburns and neck hair is recommended. Also, skin is skin whether you're male or female. So, moisturize your whole body after every shower. Plus, wear a deodorant that doesn't make you smell like a gardenia patch. All right, you're ready to go. But not so fast. I know you forgot something. Run back in and make sure you cleaned all your hair out of the sink . . . girlfriends and wives hate it!

Accessories

Every real man's man knows that the finishing touches to looking like a man's man are the accessories. Accessories set the rookies apart from the hall of famers. In this section, we are going to cover cuff links, watches, ties, jewelry, and more. We ain't talking charm bracelets here! If you've got a diamond-studded dollar sign that weighs more than a porterhouse steak hanging around your neck, you can close this book right now. A man's man is subtle. He can certainly buy expensive things, but he does not try to advertise them on the Channel 2 News.

Whether you're with coworkers, at a family function, or on a date, the people you're keeping company with will definitely notice when you're wearing a nice watch or tie. It can start conversation and break the ice at a business meeting. It lets your date know that you have fine taste in jewelry (something she knows you can apply later when shopping for her). I'm gonna give you the rundown so you know what's up. Remember, nothing too flashy, but nothing cheap. Cubic zirconia doesn't exist in the world of a man's man.

Cuff Links

Cuff links are an important part of what makes a suit look great. I would suggest buying a nice pair made of black onyx and silver; I have seen some great pairs in silver with a blue stone as well. There are, of course, expensive and less expensive options. But, no matter the price, the cuff links should complement your ensemble. Choose a pair that have something special about them, because if they catch your eye, they are bound to catch others'. If anything, I would suggest buying one great pair and wearing them to your heart's content. A lot of men think people don't notice these small details, but they do. A sharp pair of shiny cuff links might catch the eye of a prospective love interest, you never know. (No need to thank me when you walk down that aisle with your beautiful bride.)

Money Clip

Only babies keep their cash and cards in a Velcro-strip wallet and I don't baby-sit. So, throw that wallet out! Ladies, if your guy has a fanny pack . . . proceed to the nearest exit. Shoving your cash in your pocket crumpled and loose with no form of a holder is a "no can do" as well. I suggest a nice money clip, which are sold all over. You can get either a leather, gold, or sterling silver clip. Any way you go, your cash will be kept neat and stylish. If you want to kick it up a notch, I suggest getting a silver money clip engraved with your initials. When you pull it out you'll automatically look well put-together, cash and cards in tow. If you're out with your lady friend on an important date, you don't want your cash falling all over the place. Some morons just don't seem to get it . . .

Dear Frank,

There was this real pretty girl who I was trying to get a date with for months. Finally, she agreed to go out with me for dinner. I felt like this was my big night. After some great conversation, drinks and a nice meal, the bill came. When I went to pull out my credit card, all of my stuff came flying out of my pocket, including a free drink card from a go-go bar that I had gone to the night before when I was out with the guys from the office. When my date tried to help me pick up all my stuff, she saw the go-go bar card. Needless to say, the rest of the night was a disaster. She never returned any of my phone calls or emails for a second date. I really blew it. How can I get her back?

Larry

* * *

Dear Lap Dance Larry,

First of all, if you knew you were having a date with a "potential girlfriend type," you should have had all your bases covered: nicely pressed shirt and pants, clean car, and a shaven face all mean nothing if she knows you go to strip clubs. Most guys go to them, but they certainly don't advertise it to their dates. Get a money clip. And next time, throw out the free drink pass from that go-go bar—don't be cheap!

Frank

Shades

The correct shades are key. Whether you are cruising around in your ride or just going for a walk on a nice sunny day, you need the correct eyewear. Never, I repeat *never*, buy shades without trying them on first. Just because they look good in the case at the department store doesn't mean they are going to complement your face. Fit, comfort, and sleekness are the keys to a great pair of sunglasses. Try on a few pairs; don't be lazy about this. I know a lot of guys don't enjoy trying things on. But "a buy without try" is never a smart move. Also, buying a pair of shades from a street vendor is not something a true man's man does. Invest in a nice pair of quality shades that can take you from the boardroom to the beach and back again. If you don't know what looks good on your face, ask the helpful person at your local department store. With these hints you'll be looking like a stud.

Tie/Handkerchief

I like to wear ties that have a little pizazz to them, a little something that makes me stand apart from my crew. I always buy quality silk ties and I suggest you do the same. I have seen great ties for as little as $40 and upwards of $200. Listen, just because a tie is expensive doesn't mean it's a great tie. A smart way to make sure you're going to look good is to check out what's on the mannequins in the store. I like to see what the store puts together—it's a great way to get it together without the guesswork. Do not buy ties with animals, tigers, Looney Toons characters, or SpongeBob on them. We're talking classy, smooth, yet stylish ties that get you noticed in a good way. Not a "what the hell was he thinking?" way.

Another great way to top off a sharp suit is with a handkerchief. No, not the same kind you use when you've got bronchitis—this type of handkerchief is for looks only. Take some notes from Diddy. He always has a sharp handkerchief in his pocket. Please note, a man's man does not buy a tie and handkerchief set. Why? Because your handkerchief does not have to match your tie (but it should complement it.) My friend Dr. Dan recently wore a great custom suit to a party with a sharp cobalt blue tie and a light blue handkerchief. He looked great. If you have any questions, ask the man at your local department store to help you. That's a very easy way to get yourself looking dapper.

Car

Yes, a car is an accessory for a man's man. You do not have to be driving the best car on the block, but it definitely has to be clean at all times, especially if you're going on a date. Recently, I gave a friend of mine a ride to the airport. He got in my car and said to me, "Frank, it's so clean in here." I replied, "Really? It's the dirtiest it's been in six months." You see, people notice. Now, what I suggest is that a man's man has an everyday car and a weekend car. The everyday car is something he drives to work, parks on the street; most important, it should get good gas mileage. With gas prices today, you gotta watch your money clip, fellas. But the weekend car should be something sporty, like a convertible for taking your lovely lady to the country, or your buddies to the shore. Once again, whatever car you have has to be clean! I am talking no gum wrappers, coffee or soda containers, empty cigarette packs, etc. Also, no fashion magazines left in the backseat from when you gave your sister a ride. Your girlfriend will think either you're cheating on her or you're gay. The car is a reflection of you, and you're a man's man . . . so smarten up!

Watch

As I said before, a quality timepiece is key. But remember, a man's man does not need five watches. Quality, not quantity, is the key when watch hunting. If you need to save up for one then save, and when you're ready to buy a man's man–type of watch, buy just one great one—treat yourself to what you have always wanted. Besides, too many possessions just clutter your life. Now, I'm not going to name brands here, because each guy has different tastes and a watch is a personal choice. Just buy a watch that makes you feel good— you'll know it when you see it. (However, if you're looking in Chinatown, you're in the wrong place, son.) Also, make sure it's waterproof before you swan-dive into the pool.

Jewelry

Some people think that a man's man doesn't wear jewelry. That's total hogwash. I'm not saying to overdo it like some guido from Benson-hurt wearing more chains than they have in the Diamond District; what I am saying is to add a few touches of jewelry to make your look shine. A lot of men are into bracelets—I wear one, too. You could wear a cool box chain necklace, or a nice cross. Once again, quality over quantity is the key here. Another cool man's man accent is a pinky ring. Get your initials engraved in it. Have fun! *Also, a married man always wears a wedding ring.* It's a great way to profess your love. (But be sure to have one made that looks different.) Just an FYI, if you have a body piercing, that's fine. I just don't want to know where it's located!

With this helpful information, you will be looking so hot that every supermodel around the globe will be hunting you down! OK, maybe that's a little delusional. But a man's man certainly likes to aim high. In closing, let me repeat: Keep your jewelry, watch, car and everything else on this list looking spic and span at all times. You want your accessories to look like they did the day you bought them. That says a lot about you as a person. A man's man takes the time to maintain his belongings. Hey, you worked hard to get them, so why not take care of them?

Okay, I think you've gotten the point. But there's one important thing I have to mention before I stop: Don't forget that underneath all the fancy clothes, cologne, hair gel, and moisturizer is . . . *YOU.* Without a winning personality and a positive attitude, all the other stuff is a waste. A man's man never loses sight of that.

Epilogue

Congratulations! You read the whole book. So, how does it feel to enter into man's manhood? Good, right? I bet you feel like you're ready to take on the whole world. But just slow down for a second, partner. Before you head back into the big bad world with all your newfound confidence, we need to have a sit-down and discuss the most important part of this book. Now, listen up closely, because I got the mike and have something very important to say. Being a man's man is certainly about what's between the covers of this book, but that's not what it's all about. You can be staying at one of the hot Las Vegas hotels I listed, wearing one of the hand-tailored designer suits I suggested, smoking one of the top cigars I recommended, but *that alone does not* make you a man's man. What makes you a man's man is *you*! What do I mean? It's about how you handle all the situations that come your way in life. It's about treating the bellhop at the Bellagio with as much respect as its owners. It's about treating the bus driver who is sitting on your left at the cigar store with the same respect as the CEO who's sitting on your right. A man's man can be wearing the best clothes, sitting in the most expensive restaurant, drinking the finest wine (with the most beautiful woman on his arm), but if he doesn't treat everyone around him with respect and class, then he is *not* a real man's man. He's just a jerkoff in a good suit.

Sure, there was some humor in this book. We made fun of some people, places, and things. But, seriously, a man's man is always going to take control of himself and do the right thing when put into certain situations. He always takes a moment to think about his actions before he does anything rash and realizes that his actions have consequences and could possibly hurt or offend others. He leaves a good impression on everyone he meets. His success is his friends' and family's success. He never loses his head no matter how "big" he gets. I will never forget something that happened in my life some years back. An actor friend of mine (I'm not gonna name names) was having a tough time getting a job. He would call me every day asking me for my advice, support, and help. Being the man's man that I take pride in being, I never turned my back on him. No matter how busy I was, I would always take his phone call, lend my ear, and give him solid advice. Remember, being an actor is tough—you have more moments of self-doubt and insecurity than people in a lot of other professions. All day long you hear stuff like, "You're too tall, too short, too old, too young, etc." But, I would always encourage my friend to push forward. Sure enough, one day I read in *Variety* that he was cast in a big new television series. I was so happy for him. I immediately picked up the phone to congratulate him on his new success. When he answered the phone, he coldly said, "Frank, I'm way too busy to talk. I have to memorize a script and prepare for this new part. In fact, I am going to be way too busy to talk for quite a while. I'll call you." Then, he hung up on me. I said to myself, "What!?" I was completely dumbfounded. The guy changed overnight. I was always there for him, supporting him when he needed me. That's what a man's man does for his friends. The moral of this story? No matter how successful you get, you should never lose your head, because the ones who lose their heads fall the hardest.

Fellas, it's going to be a long journey until you accomplish all of your dreams and goals in life. However, along the way, a true man's man never forgets the people who believed in and supported him. If good things happen quickly for you in life, well then, that's great. If things are not moving as quickly as you would like them to, you must analyze the situation closely. If there's something really out of whack or amiss in his life, a man's man takes a step back and really looks at what's going on. Take control of the situation by remembering that control starts with you. Here are a few more man's man pearls of wisdom: Don't take all your interactions with other people personally. The only people you take personally are family and close friends. In a lifetime, you should only accumulate as many close friends as you can count on one hand. Also, never take business relations personally.

And remember this one saying: "Great spirits have always encountered violent opposition from mediocre minds." Apply what's in this book, add your own good judgment, and no matter what, never lose sight of yourself. That's the way you become a man's man. And when you're a real man's man, the world can be yours!

Frank Vincent
Filmography

A Shark Tale (2004)—Great
  White #3
Remedy (2003)—Johnnie
  Marandino
A Tale of Two Pizzas (2003)—Frank
  Bianco
This Things of Ours (2003)—Danny
  Santini
Rubout (2003)—Frank Santello
The Last Request (2002)—Father
  Bryce
Grand Theft Auto III (2001)—
  D. Salvatore Leone
Snipes (2001)—Johnnie Marandino
Smokin' Stogies (2001)—Johnny Big
Under Hellgate Bridge (2000)—Big
  Sal

The Crew (2000)—Marty
Ropewalk (2000)—Angelo
If You Only Knew (2000)—Gino
Gun Shy (2000)—Carmine Minetti
Isn't She Great (2000)—Aristotle
  Onassis
Entropy (1999)—Sal
NetForce (1999)—Tommy
Undercurrent (1998)—Eddie Torelli
Vig (1998)—Pete
Belly (1998)—Roger
The North End (1998)—Dom Di
  Bella
Witness to the Mob (1998)—Frankie
  DeCicco
Made Men (1997)—Tommy "The
  Bull" Vitaglia

The Deli (1997)—Tommy
Cop Land (1997)—Vincent Lassaro
Grind (1997)—Nick
Night Falls on Manhattan (1997)—
   Captain
Nothing to Lose (1996)—Ray
   Digovanni, Sr.
West New York (1996)—Tom
   Colletti
She's the One (1996)—
   Renee's dad
Gotti (1996)—Robert DiBernardo
Lou, Pat & Joe D (1995)—Pop
   Corelli
Casino (1995)—Frank Marino
Federal Hill (1994)—Sal
Hand Gun (1994)—Earl
Men Lie (1994)—Uncle Frank
*Dead and Alive: The Race for Gus
   Farace (1991)*—Joseph F.
   Zanni Jr.
Jungle Fever (1991)—Mike Tucci
Mortal Thoughts (1991)—Dominic
   Marino
Street Hunter (1990)—Don Mario
   Romano
Goodfellas (1990)—Billy Batts
Last Exit to Brooklyn (1989)—Priest

Do the Right Thing (1989)—
   Charlie
Wise Guys (1986)—Louie Fontucci
*The Pope of Greenwich Village
   (1984)*—1st Crew Chief
Easy Money (1983)—Paulie
Baby It's You (1983)—Vinnie
Dear Mr. Wonderful (1982)—Louie
Raging Bull (1980)—Salvy
The Death Collector (1975)—Bernie
   Feldshuh

Notable TV Show
Appearances

The Sopranos (2004–Present)—Phil
   Leotardo
NYPD Blue (1993)—Dino "The
   Rat" Ferrera (recurring)
Law & Order (1990)—Jon
   Franchetta
Cosby (1996)
Walker, Texas Ranger (1993)—Paul
   Mancini
*The Young Indiana Jones Chronicles
   (1992)*
Law & Order (1990)—J.Z.

Photo Credits

Frank Vincent is an actor, musician, writer and producer. One only has to see him at work in classic movies like *Raging Bull, Do the Right Thing*, and *Casino* to be convinced of his versatility. His passion for music and playing the drums led to a successful career as a recording drummer for such prominent names as arranger Don Costa, as well as singers Paul Anka and Trini Lopez. As an actor, Vincent debuted in 1975 in Ralph DeVito's *Death Collector*, where he impressed director Martin Scorsese with his on-screen work. Scorsese cast him in the Academy Award–nominated film *Raging Bull* and the rest is cinematic history. Vincent has gone on to appear in over fifty feature films. In addition to Scorsese, he has worked for some of the greatest directors of our time, including Brian DePalma, Spike Lee and Sidney Lumet. He plays the parts audiences remember long after they leave the theater. In fact, who could forget him as the infamous Billy Batts in *Goodfellas*, where he tells Joe Pesci's character to "Go home and get your shinebox!" Most recently, you can see Vincent in the starring role of Phil Leotardo on *The Sopranos*. His voice is also featured in the multimillion dollar Playstation video game series Grand Theft Auto as the character "Don Salvatore Leone." In 2002, he received the Italian-American Entertainer of the Year Award, presented by the *Italian Tribune* and in 2005 he was the recipient of the Garden State Film Festival Lifetime Achievement Award for Acting. Check out his website at www.frankvincent.com.

Steven Priggé has written three previous books. He is the coauthor of the Italian-American celebrity cookbook *Shut Up and Eat!*, and the author of *Movie Moguls Speak* and *Created By*. Priggé also writes freelance articles for such popular publications as *Bon Appétit, Budget Living, MovieMaker, Scr(i)pt*, and *Written By*. Visit his website at www.stevenprigge.com.